ENCOUNT

Encounters with God

Some Lesser Known Characters of the New Testament

Peter Williams

EVANGELICAL PRESS OF WALES

© Evangelical Press of Wales, 1996
First published 1996
ISBN 1 85049 121 6

Cover photo by T. David Carey-Jones
Cover design& illustrations by Rhiain M. Davies (Cain)

Published by the Evangelical Press of Wales
Bryntirion, Bridgend CF31 4DX, Wales, UK
Printed by Bridgend Print Centre, Bridgend

Contents

To my dear wife
Brenda who has been my
greatest help in the work of ministry

Introduction

These character studies are based on a series of sermons preached to the morning congregation of Moordown Baptist Church during 1993. They were well received at the time and many were kind enough to say that the studies helped them to feel that the people of the New Testament were 'real' people with the same strengths and weaknesses we all share.

I hope this book will help others to see that human nature is essentially the same from age to age and that the only lasting change for the better is that brought about by the power of God in the Lord Jesus Christ. It may also help those engaged in preaching and teaching the Word of God to adopt a realistic approach to their ministry and not always to expect a ready response to the gospel. We must not be deceived by the innate goodness in man nor on the other hand despair at the hardness of the human heart to spiritual concerns.

Ours is to set forth the greatness of Christ and his gospel and to leave the final issue with God.

I wish to express my deep thanks to my friend and colleague David Cheadle for his help in preparing the manuscript for publication.

Peter Williams
Bournemouth 1996

1
Sergius Paulus
a thinking man

Read Acts 13:4-12

The background to the conversion of Sergius Paulus to the Christian faith is the first missionary journey of Paul and Barnabas, who were sent out by the church at Antioch (13:1-3). Their first stopping place was Cyprus where they preached the Word of God through the whole island, arriving eventually at Paphos, the centre of Roman government.

An intelligent man

Here they met Sergius Paulus, an eminent statesman and public figure, who was the proconsul or governor of the island. He is described as an intelligent man (v.7), which is simply another way of saying that he was a thinking man and an enquirer after truth. He was a man of prominence and position enjoying a good life-style, but at the same time he seems to have been seeking something above all that, something higher than the material and political world in which he moved.

Sergius Paulus was in fact reaching out for some kind of spiritual understanding and in that sense he represents all those in our day who are thinking people seeking answers to the meaning and purpose of life. That is why he had as a member of his staff a Jewish sorcerer named Bar-Jesus or Elymas (v.6,7). In the eyes of the governor Elymas represented spiritual reality, but it was of the wrong kind. He was an agent of pagan occult powers and as a Jewish prophet he would have had a knowledge of the Old Testament scriptures which he distorted and perverted to promote his own false teaching. Paul saw through him immediately: 'You are a child of the devil and an enemy of everything that is right! You are full of all kinds of deceit and trickery. Will you never stop perverting the right ways of the Lord?' (v.10)

At this point in his life Sergius Paulus knew nothing of spiritual truth beyond the Satanic influence of Elymas. And that is saying two things to us. Firstly, it shows that all men have a spiritual dimension to their nature. We are more than mere flesh and bone, mind and intellect. There is a spiritual dimension to the human personality which the Bible calls the soul. Sergius Paulus, like many today, held a good position which met his intellectual and material needs but which did not truly satisfy him or keep him from seeking spiritual answers to the great issues of life. Secondly, because God made man a spiritual being it means he cannot help but search for spiritual truth and reality even if, like Sergius Paulus, he mistakenly looks in the wrong direction of a man like Elymas. That is largely the explanation of the popularity of New Age philosophy and the growing interest in astrology, spiritism, witchcraft, black magic, satanism and all the pseudo-religions and cults springing up today. Where there is a spiritual vacuum in people's lives, they will seek to fill it in whatever way they can.

Open to the Word of God

The great change came about for Sergius Paulus when he heard of the preaching of Paul and Barnabas. 'The Proconsul, an intelligent man, sent for Barnabas and Paul because he wanted to hear the Word of God' (v.7). By sending for the Christian missionaries the Governor was showing that he was genuinely seeking the truth of God and the Scriptures are clear that God always loves a true seeker. 'You will seek me and find me when you seek me with all your heart' (Jeremiah 29:13). God always honours that man or woman who is seeking salvation and that is why he made it possible for Sergius Paulus to hear his Word through the preaching of Barnabas and Paul.

For the thinking person who knows in his heart that there is more to the understanding of life than what satisfies him materially and intellectually, God will open up a way for him to become acquainted with the truth of his Word either through a sermon, or tract, or a book or the personal witness of a friend or colleague or in some other way. When that happens the next step is then up to that person. The Lord Jesus said: '. . . he who seeks finds' (Matthew 7:8).

Hindrances to faith

But no sooner had Sergius Paulus heard the truth of the gospel from the lips of Barnabas and Paul, than Elymas the sorcerer intervened to hinder the Governor from coming to faith in Christ. 'Elymas the sorcerer . . . opposed them and tried to turn the proconsul from the faith' (v.8).

Here was the clash of spiritual powers that the New Testament talks so much about (Ephesians 6:12). On the one hand the power of God's Holy Spirit was working through Paul: on the other hand, the principalities and powers of darkness were present in Elymas. What was at stake in the battle was the immortal soul of Sergius Paulus. Elymas knew that if the Governor was converted to faith in the Lord Jesus

Christ then it was all over with him and the cause of evil he represented. But Paul in the power of the Holy Spirit dealt with him very effectively. ' "Now the hand of the Lord is against you. You are going to be blind, and for a time you will be unable to see the light of the sun." Immediately mist and darkness came over him, and he groped about, seeking someone to lead him by the hand' (v.11).

This spiritual warfare for the souls of men and women is going on all the time in our world. Satan hates the seeker for God's truth and will use trickery, deceit and falsity of every kind to prevent and hinder a person from receiving God's Word and entering into God's salvation. In the soul of that person God says: 'I gave my Son as a sacrifice for your sin. Trust me for salvation and come into my Kingdom.' At the same time Satan says: 'Don't believe it. It's all stuff and nonsense this talk about sin and the need for salvation. You are neither better nor worse than anyone else. Forget it.' So the battle rages.

Believing in Christ

Clearly the battle for the soul of Sergius Paulus was lost by Satan that day and the power of God proved greater, for we read: 'When the proconsul saw what had happened, he believed, for he was amazed at the teaching about the Lord' (v.12).

He saw the evidence of the Holy Spirit's work in what happened to Elymas and he entrusted his immortal soul and destiny to the keeping of Almighty God. He also heard the 'teaching' of the gospel from Paul and Barnabas. We must never forget that these two things always go together. Proclamation of the truth and practice of the truth are the twin pillars of effective witness to God.

2
Demas
the backslider

Read 2 Timothy 4:10-18

In this passage Paul gives a list of his fellow-workers in
the gospel and items of information concerning them.
First in the list is Demas and what Paul says about him is
terribly sad. It is only one sentence but it speaks volumes
about the man. 'Do your best to come to me quickly, for
Demas, because he loved this world, has deserted me and
has gone to Thessalonica' (v.9,10).

Desertion is a form of betrayal. It is turning one's back
upon someone especially in the time of crisis when they need
our help and support. Paul was in a cold prison cell writing
this letter, shortly to face his second trial and possible death.
He needed the Christian brethren to stand by him but where
Demas was concerned he was let down in the same way as
our Lord on the night of his crucifixion when we are told that
'everyone deserted him and fled' (Mark 14:50). What hurt
Paul most of all was the reason Demas deserted him—
'because he loved this world'. That is why we describe him
as a backslider, because he deserted not only Paul but the
Lord Jesus Christ. He is mentioned in two other places. 'Our
dear friend Luke, the doctor, and Demas send greetings'
(Colossians 4:14). '. . . Demas and Luke, my fellow-workers
(Philemon v.24). Clearly at that time he loved the Lord and

13

was active in Christian work. What caused him to desert Christ?

Citizen of two worlds

We must keep in mind that the Christian believer is a citizen of two worlds and there is always a conflict between our love for the one and the other. Millions know and love only 'this' world with its loves and joys, its hates and pleasures. We should not envy them because this can be a pretty rotten world at times. Let's face it, life for many people can be very bleak. It is a world of violence, war and suffering; a world of unemployment, hardship and disillusionment for many. So if this is the only world we know and love, we are not to be envied.

The Christian too, lives in this world, sharing in its joys and pleasures. But he knows and loves the other eternal world in the presence of God to which in Christ he is drawing closer every day. Paul says: '. . . our citizenship is in heaven' (Philippians 3:20). He means that whilst we belong to a nation and people in this world of time, our true home is in eternity where God dwells. There is an old saying: 'The world is a bridge; the wise man will cross over it but will not build his house upon it.' The believer is only passing through this world and he will see everything in this life against the backcloth of eternity.

In this way the believer is able to keep the things of this world in perspective and will not allow them to govern and control his life. It seems that Demas had forgotten all that and had allowed this world, and the things of this world, to seduce him from his love for Christ and the hope of heaven. That is a temptation for all of us, for, although a person enters into a new life in Christ when he becomes a Christian, at the same time he has to live that new life in this sinful world. The result is a battle between the two worlds to which he now belongs. More than that, although the Holy Spirit now resides in him, he still has to contend with his old sinful nature and therefore the battle is carried on within the personality. The hymn puts it like this:

> *Just as I am, though tossed about*
> *With many a conflict, many a doubt,*
> *Fightings and fears within, without,*
> *O Lamb of God, I come.*

Demas clearly lost the battle.

Where does our love lie?

But where does our love really lie? Is it towards the new world of God's kingdom to which we now belong, or to the things of this world? John mentions the things of this world which can so easily entice the believer to backslide from the love of Christ. 'Do not love the world or anything in the world. If anyone loves the world, the love of the Father is not in him. For everything in the world—the cravings of sinful man, the lust of his eyes and the boasting of what he has and does—comes not from the Father but from the world. The world and its desires pass away, but the man who does the will of God lives for ever' (1 John 2:15-17).

Notice the things John mentions. He speaks first of all of 'the cravings of sinful man'. What are the cravings? All the things that pander to our appetites and indulgences and which encourage a worldly spirit: the inordinate love of ease and pleasure, the extravagance of fashion, the love of possessions, the gratification of personal desires. In short, craving for a soft and flabby moral approach to life which thinks only of self and which we see so much of today.

Then there is 'the lust of his eyes'. He means that covetous, discontented spirit which is always wanting more and is always envious of what it sees others have. It means to be enticed by the outward glamour and superficialities of life in this world whilst ignoring the realities of the things which are eternal.

Thirdly, he speaks of 'the boasting of what he has and does'. Nothing characterizes our modern world more than man's pride. Pride in cleverness, achievements, technology and science, so that man has no sense of need. He doesn't need God, faith, the Bible, prayer, forgiveness or salvation. Modern man's pride has cut himself off from the mercy and grace of God and the result is the miserable state of our world today.

In all this John is warning us against being enticed by the false glamour of this world in the way that Demas fell in love with it and deserted the cause of Christ.

It can happen to us

The frightening thing is that we can become infected so easily by this world of ours. We can get sucked into the pagan environment with its false values and standards and sophisticated behaviour. When Demas worked with Paul in the gospel I doubt if he ever felt that he would one day desert the cause of Christ. Perhaps when he visited Paul in prison in Rome the glamour and life-style of the great city cast its spell over him and almost unconsciously captivated his heart so that Paul had to say sadly: 'Demas, because he loved this world, has deserted me.'

To prevent that happening to us we have to be on our guard against the 'wiles of the devil'. John says that 'the whole world is under the control of the evil one' (1 John 5:19). If we are to counteract his controlling power then we must daily bring our lives more and more under the control and direction of the Holy Spirit. 'Don't let the world around you squeeze you into its own mold, but let God remold your minds from within' (Romans 12:2 J. B. Phillips).

3
Felix
who missed his opportunity

Read Acts 24:22-27

Felix was the Roman Governor before whom Paul stood trial to face certain accusations brought against him by the Jewish leaders (24:1). Quite a lot is known about Felix from sources outside the Bible. Josephus the Jewish historian and Tacitus the Roman historian describe him as an unprincipled and corrupt official who would stoop to anything, however low, to fulfil his own ambitions. Even the brief account in Acts reveals his greed for money—'he was hoping that Paul would offer him a bribe' (v.26), and his total disregard for justice—'because Felix wanted to grant a favour to the Jews, he left Paul in prison' (v.27).

His personal life was one of open contempt for morality. He was married three times, on each occasion to a royal princess. His third wife Drusilla (v.24) was a Jewess, who in fact was living in adultery with Felix since she was already married to Azizus, King of Emesa. Eventually, in about AD 58, Felix's political scandals and corruptions took him a step too far and he was recalled to Rome and dismissed from office. That was the man who was to pass judgment on the great apostle Paul.

People of the Way

We are told in verse 22 that Felix 'was well acquainted with the Way'. That was an early description of Christianity. The first believers were called people of the Way (Acts 9:2; 24:14), because they followed the Lord Jesus Christ who claimed to be the only way into the presence of God. 'I am the way and the truth and the life. No-one comes to the Father except through me' (John 14:6). This tells us that, in the final analysis, the Christian message is not about a philosophy, or a system of ethics, or a blue-print for living, but about a personal relationship with the Lord Jesus. He is the way from God to man by revealing to us the knowledge and understanding of God, and he is the way from man to God by providing through his own sacrifice on the cross a means of reconciliation with God.

Acquaintance with Christianity

When we read that Felix 'was well acquainted with the Way', that is simply saying that he had a working knowledge of Christianity and its message. We have no information as to how, as a Gentile and a pagan, he came by that knowledge. It may have been through his wife Drusilla who, as a Jewess, may have come into contact with the early believers. The sad thing was that Felix's acquaintance with the gospel was only head knowledge. He knew nothing of the inner experience of God's love and forgiveness in the Lord Jesus Christ.

That is true of a good many people—they have an acquaintance with the truth of God and may even be able to discuss the Bible, to use evangelical language, and yet it is evident from what they say, that it is no more than an intellectual understanding which does not penetrate below the level of the mind. Such people will often spend hours discussing 'religion' because they are fascinated with the elemental and mysterious issues it raises. Herod was like that with John the Baptist. 'When Herod heard John, he was greatly puzzled; yet he liked to listen to him' (Mark 6:20).

Felix may have been of the same turn of mind because, apart from hearing Paul at the trial, it seems he sent for the apostle for a personal interview. 'He sent for Paul and listened to him as he spoke about faith in Christ Jesus (v.24). What is more, these personal conversations about Christianity were held frequently during the two years of Paul's imprisonment although Felix's motives were mixed with personal greed. 'He was hoping that Paul would offer him a bribe, so he sent for him frequently and talked with him' (v.26). The truth was that Felix was a mixed-up man and a rather pathetic figure. In spite of his corrupt and licentious life and in spite of the fallen depraved state of mankind generally, there is that wistful longing for God that breaks through the surface of a man's life from time to time. The writer of Ecclesiastes puts it well: 'He has also set eternity in the hearts of men; yet they cannot fathom what God has done from beginning to end' (3:11).

A frightened man

Felix was interested and fascinated with what Paul had to say about the gospel of Christ until, that is, he got down to the nitty-gritty of things. 'As Paul discoursed on righteousness, self-control and the judgment to come, Felix was afraid and said, "That's enough for now! You may leave..."' (v.25). Perhaps that shows more than anything else that Felix was interested in the gospel mainly at the intellectual level. Once it dealt with his life-style, the need for holiness of life and self-discipline and the judgment of God, it made him feel deeply uneasy and he wanted to hear no more. In place of the word 'afraid', the Authorized Version says that 'Felix trembled'. With a life like his who wouldn't tremble at the thought of meeting God at the Judgment?

The Church's message

That raises the question: Does the Church in her preaching today ever make men and women tremble? There were three elements to Paul's message that would do that and help to make people aware of God and to worship him 'acceptably with reverence and awe' (Hebrews 12:28).

Firstly, he spoke of the need for personal righteousness. That simply means that a man or a woman needs to be put right with God. But how can a man who is sinful be put right with God or be reconciled to a person who is altogether pure and holy? That is what made Felix tremble when he looked at the rotten sinful state of his own heart. He knew that he had no hope of ever being right with God.

Secondly, he spoke of the need for self-control and discipline in a person's life. That made Felix afraid when he thought of his own infidelities and corruptions. We have only to look at the breakdown in discipline in our homes and schools and society in general, and the way in which passion and lust seem to rule and govern the lives of so many, to realize how angry God must be with our nation. But if there is no godliness or righteousness, how can it be otherwise? In the life of any society the breakdown in personal morality and the increase in wickedness is always preceded by godlessness or a lack of righteousness. 'The wrath of God is being revealed . . . against all the godlessness and wickedness of men' (Romans 1:18).

The third element in Paul's message was that he spoke of the judgment to come and the fact that men are accountable to a holy God at the last. That surely caused Felix to tremble and to be afraid. The Word of God clearly says: 'Everything is uncovered and laid bare before the eyes of him to whom we must give account' (Hebrews 4:13). The Church in its message must remind people that, at the end of the day when we leave this world, we shall do so stripped naked of everything but our immortal souls and the record of the life lived below, and that we shall stand before God at the Judgment.

The missed opportunity

The fact that Felix was afraid or trembled as he listened to Paul was a sign that the Holy Spirit was disturbing and convicting his soul. If only in that moment, when his eyes were being opened to the way in which sin and greed were dominating his life, he had responded by repenting and by putting his faith in Christ, how different his life would have become. Instead, he cut Paul short: 'When I find it convenient, I will send for you'. He did indeed send for him frequently over the next two years, but the convenient moment for the breakthrough in faith never came. Never again did the Holy Spirit cause Felix to be 'afraid' of God and the Judgment. He missed his opportunity, the moment passed and the old hardness of heart returned. There is only one convenient moment and it is 'now': 'now is the time of God's favour, now is the day of salvation' (2 Corinthians 6:2).

4
Gamaliel
a tolerant man

Read Acts 5:34-42

Peter and the other apostles were in deep trouble. They had been brought before the Sanhedrin or Jewish Supreme Council for daring to preach publicly the gospel of Jesus Christ. When warned by the authorities to give up this evangelistic activity Peter, the chief spokesman, replied: 'We must obey God rather than men' (5:29). This only served to worsen their situation and some members of the Council began clamouring for their death (v.33). It was at this point that Gamaliel, a prominent member of the Council, began to make his presence felt.

Gamaliel—who was he?

'But a Pharisee named Gamaliel, a teacher of the law, who was honoured by all the people, stood up in the Sanhedrin and ordered that the men be put outside for a little while' (v.34). Clearly Gamaliel was a good and godly man who was held in the highest regard by everyone, including his fellow-members on the Council. He was also a distinguished scholar and teacher of God's law and at one time had actually taught the apostle Paul in his pre-Christian student days. 'Then Paul said . . . "Under Gamaliel I was thoroughly trained in the law of our fathers and was just as zealous for

God as any of you are today"' (Acts 22:3). This is the man we are now considering and who addresses the Council on behalf of the apostles.

You can't beat God

He reminds the Council that prior to the movement led by Peter and the other apostles there had been similar movements and uprisings in Israel before, and they had come to nothing. He gives two instances. Theudas led a popular uprising with four hundred men but eventually he was killed and the whole thing petered out. Then a Galilean named Judas set himself up as a national deliverer with a group of followers, but he, too, was killed and it all came to nothing (v.35-7). Gamaliel then warns the Council: 'Therefore, in the present case I advise you: Leave these men alone! Let them go! For if their purpose or activity is of human origin, it will fail. But if it is from God, you will not be able to stop these men; you will only find yourselves fighting against God' (v.38,39).

That was wise advice and it is perfectly true still. You can't beat God! You can't fight against God and hope to win! But that was precisely the mistake the Jewish leaders were making in opposing Peter and the other apostles. They thought that they were up against a group of ignorant fishermen with a half-brained scheme called the 'Way' with which they hoped to change the world. They didn't realize that behind Peter and the apostles there was the eternal God and all the forces and powers of heaven. They didn't stand a chance of winning. The proof of that lies in the very existence of the Church today and the gospel it preaches.

The opposition and hositility of secular world powers against the Church today is extremely powerful but we always have the promise of the Lord Jesus, 'I will build my church, and the gates of hell will not overcome it' (Matthew

16:18). Picture something like this. Imagine the gates of hell being thrown wide open and all the demonic powers under the leadership of Satan storming out intent on destroying the work of God in the Church and in the preaching of the gospel of salvation. They attempt to overcome through persecution and distress brought upon the Church by rulers, governments, dictators and totalitarian states. Often in her history the Church has been brought low, but never has she been overcome. As J. C. Ryle said, 'In spite of everything, her own failures, falls and shortcomings, in spite of the world, the flesh and the devil, the cause of God has been, and will be victorious, and every true believer in the Lord Jesus Christ will be brought home to heaven at last and to glory and life everlasting.'

Gamaliel was absolutely right. You can't fight God and hope to win.

Tolerant to all

We commend Gamaliel for what he said therefore, but I am not so sure that we can go further than that. In his case it is a question of 'Do what I say, but do not do what I do'. He spoke up on behalf of the apostles not because he was anxious to defend the cause of Christ. In fact he ordered that the apostles should leave the court before he made his speech (v.34). That is, he didn't want them to think that he was identifying with them simply because he was speaking on their behalf. And yet he pleads with the court to set them free.

In this respect Gamaliel represents a lot of people in the Church today—those who like to regard themselves as being very tolerant and broadminded and moderate in all things, even Christian things. We can't help noticing Gamaliel's use of the word 'if' in his speech—'if it is of God' (v.39). He says in effect: 'Now we must be tolerant in all this, after all there might be something in this Christian movement. We mustn't think that we are the only ones to have knowledge of the truth. No, we must see it from their point of view and try to be broadminded. Toleration in all things, that's my advice.'

All this has a familiar and modern ring about it. Living as we are in a multi-faith society, we have Church leaders telling us that we must be tolerant of one another and learn to accept each other's faith as a part of the total revelation of God to mankind. 'After all', they say, 'there are many roads leading to God.' And in this way the distinctives of the gospel are set aside. The uniqueness of Christ as the Way, the Truth and the Life is completely lost. And didn't Christ himself say: 'No-one comes to the Father except through me.' But if we dare proclaim the uniqueness of Christ as Saviour and Lord, one is immediately accused of being intolerant, bigoted, narrow-minded and insensitive. Whereas in fact, this Gamaliel approach in Christian things is often only an excuse for a lack of real conviction concerning God's revelation in the person of the Lord Jesus Christ.

There is a wrong kind of tolerance in which we accept *everything* and believe *nothing*. There is also a right kind of intolerance where we express our own firm convictions and disagreements with others but at the same time allow them the right to their own beliefs.

The peril of neutrality

Because he was so concerned with wanting to be thought tolerant and broadminded, Gamaliel did nothing positive with regard to the gospel of salvation being preached by Peter and the other apostles. His advice to the court was, 'Leave these men alone! Let them go!' In other words, 'Don't oppose them, but don't support them either. Just don't get involved. Leave it where it is.' He was advocating a non-interventionist policy. It reminds us of the words of Pilate's wife at the trial of Jesus: 'Don't have anything to do with that innocent man' (Matthew 27:19). She didn't want to do anything against Jesus but she didn't do anything for him either!

There are thousands who adopt this non-interventionist policy where Christ is concerned. They do not oppose the gospel, but neither do they embrace it. They say in effect: 'I'm not against Christianity. In fact, I'm quite tolerant of all religions. If you want to get enthusiastic about sin and forgiveness, heaven and hell, then that's all right with me. Only let me get on with my life.' Then that same person immerses himself in the business of daily living with its commitments and pleasures, fondly imagining that he is being decent and broadminded and totally neutral with regard to it all.

But where God and man's immortal destiny are concerned, there is no such thing as neutrality or 'not getting involved'. We *are* already involved, whether we like it or not. We were involved with God from the moment he created us in our mother's womb. We are obligated to him for everything we have in this life. We cannot therefore avoid making a conscious decision with regard to what he has said and done in the gospel of salvation provided in his Son.

None of us can afford the luxury of even thinking that we can be neutral in relation to the claims of Christ. There is too much at stake—eternal life or eternal death. There are only two kingdoms, God's kingdom and Satan's kingdom. If we are not in the one, then we can only be in the other. Jesus said that there are only two roads in life, the narrow road that leads to life and the broad road that leads to destruction. The only questions that matter in the end are: whose kingdom are we in and on which road are we travelling?

5
Lydia
the first European convert

Read Acts 16:11-15

When Paul received his vision of a man calling him over to Macedonia to preach (16:9,10), he and his companions crossed the Aegean Sea to Philippi. In so doing they were taking the gospel from east to west, from Asia to Europe.

Lydia's character

On the Sabbath Paul and his companions went down to the riverside 'expecting' to find a place of prayer. They were not disappointed because Lydia and some other women were there (v.13). Philippi was a Roman colony and only a few Jews lived there, whereas Jewish law held that a minimum of ten men was necessary to establish a synagogue. In the absence of a synagogue the women held their devotions at the riverside. Lydia appears to have been an intelligent, go-ahead kind of woman who had made her mark in the business world. She came originally from Thyatira and was 'a dealer in purple cloth' (v.14). Thyatira was a centre of the purple woollen industry out of which the finest clothes were made, including garments for royalty and the nobility. It seems Lydia had made a success of her business in Philippi and was a woman of considerable means with servants and a large house, and she was able to entertain Paul and his companions (v.15).

What is significant about Lydia and the other women is that the absence of a synagogue did not prevent them from continuing their devotional and prayer life. Lydia, being the kind of woman she was, may even have taken the initiative in this. Whatever the explanation, it reminds us that in our churches we owe a great debt to the womenfolk. Often it is they and not the men who show the dynamic and initiative and drive when it comes to organizing church life and promoting the things of God. In many local churches and missionary organizations it is the women who have taken on the leadership roles, either because the men won't do it, or because they are not there to do it. Indeed, one of the gravest weaknesses on the present day Christian scene is the abdication by men of responsibility for the leadership roles both in the church and the home. It is the women like Lydia and her friends who are so often out front.

Use of resources

This picture of the women meeting for prayer at the riverside also teaches us that in God's work we do not have to wait until we have all the resources we want before we get on with that work. If there is no comfortable synagogue to worship in, there is always the riverside. It is true that both churches and individuals can be very negative in this matter of resources. 'If only we had more money, bigger and better buildings and greater facilities' seems to be the complaint of some churches. Or 'if only I were a better speaker or were more talented and had more time.' In this negative way we can deceive ourselves about what we *would* do if we had all the resources we want, but in the meantime we do nothing about it at all.

God surely is more interested in what we are doing with the resources we already have, however small and meagre. If there is no synagogue there is always the riverside and he wants us to get on with it.

The necessity of conversion

Lydia was engaged in prayer and we are told that she 'was a worshipper of God' (v.14). But she knew nothing of God's salvation until Paul preached to her and the others the gospel of Jesus Christ. It was after that we read: 'When she and the members of her household were baptized, she invited us to her home. "If you consider me a believer in the Lord," she said, "come and stay at my house"' (v.15). That tells us that many folk today are sincere in their worship, praying and giving to worthy causes and living a good moral life, but they still need to experience God's salvation through repentance and personal faith in the Lord Jesus Christ. Ask them if they believe in God and in prayer and they will say 'yes, most certainly'. But if you press them further and ask 'do you know Christ as your Saviour, does the Holy Spirit live in you, is heaven your home?' they will look bewildered and might even take offence. They dislike all this talk about their soul and the need to be 'born again'. Nevertheless they, like Lydia, in spite of their belief in God and in prayer, need to learn that salvation is found only through personal faith in the Lord Jesus Christ.

Lydia heard the gospel

But to learn of that salvation Lydia had first to hear that gospel preached. Someone had to point her to Christ. That is what Paul and his companions did: 'We sat down and began to speak to the women who had gathered there. One of those listening was a woman named Lydia' (v.13,14). What Paul spoke about was the way of God's salvation, for that is how people are brought to faith in Christ. 'Consequently, faith comes from hearing the message, and the message is heard through the word of Christ' (Romans 10:17).

There are thousands of dear folk in our churches today who are devout and sincere but who never hear the word of God's salvation preached. They are given moralistic sermons or humanistic homilies, but they are never explicitly told that we are all born in sin and are estranged from God and that there is no hope of heaven and eternal life apart from repentance and faith in the substitutionary sacrifice of the Lord Jesus Christ.

And if they are not going to hear it from our pulpits, where are they going to hear of the way of salvation?

God opened Lydia's heart

As she listened with deep earnestness to Paul's message something profound happened to Lydia. 'The Lord opened her heart to respond to Paul's message' (v.14). It all came together: Paul's faithfulness in preaching salvation, Lydia's earnestness in 'listening' to the gospel and the Holy Spirit honouring both those things in awakening Lydia to personal faith. 'If you consider me a believer in the Lord,' she said, 'come and stay at my house' (v.15).

Lydia didn't open her own heart. Nor was it Paul who did that through the eloquence of his preaching. It was the unction or anointing of the Spirit's power upon the Word preached which convicted Lydia of her sin and her need of salvation. That is why it is so important for believers to bring friends and acquaintances to gospel services for we can be sure that God is always ready and willing to open someone's heart to saving faith.

What Lydia did

We should notice in conclusion that following her conversion experience Lydia did two very positive things. First, she and the others who had come to faith in her household were baptized (v.15). It was not the baptism that made her a believer. She had already received the message of salvation in her heart. She was being baptized becase she was already a believer. Her baptism was the outward expression or witness to the fact that she had died to her old life and risen to a new life in Christ. The sacraments of Baptism and the Lord's Supper are both means of God's grace but we should never confuse them with the notion that somehow they can make us Christians by being a substitute for personal faith and the work of the Holy Spirit in the heart.

Secondly, Lydia immediately put her new-found faith into practice by opening her home and giving hospitality to Paul and his companions. More exciting is the fact that from that house group and the conversion experience of that one woman came the foundation of the church at Philippi. We never know what God will do through us when we give ourselves fully to him.

6
Epaphras
a faithful minister

Read Colossians 1:6-8; 4:12,13

All that we know about Epaphras is contained in these few verses. His name, which means 'lovely' or 'charming', is the shortened form of the Greek name Aphrodite, the goddess of love. Like many others in the New Testament, Epaphras had been brought by the power of the gospel out of the darkness of paganism into the light of God's kingdom. Following his conversion he became a fellow-worker with Paul who gives him a glowing testimony as 'our dear fellow-servant, who is a faithful minister of Christ' (1:7).

A faithful witness

It is virtually certain that Epaphras was himself a native of Colossae since Paul describes him as 'Epaphras, who is one of you' (4:12). Also it was from him that they first heard the Word of the gospel. 'All over the world this gospel is producing fruit . . . just as it has been doing among you . . . you learned it from Epaphras' (1:6,7). Before ever he pioneered a church in Colossae and became its first pastor, Epaphras therefore was a faithful witness to his own people.

Witnessing for Christ is often difficult but never more so

than when we try to speak for Christ to those we know and who are familiar with us, such as friends and family. Yet that may be the most important place to start witnessing, for they know what we were like before we became Christians and will be able to see the change that has taken place in our lives.

To be a faithful and effective witness our testimony needs to have certain ingredients. First of all, we must be able to speak from first-hand knowledge. It will not impress people to tell them that the Lord Jesus Christ is a great Saviour unless they can see that he is our Saviour and that the truth we are witnessing to has changed us and that we are willing to stake everything on it. That is especially true if we are witnessing to those who know us because they are able to compare our lives with what they were before and see the reality of what it is we are saying.

Secondly, our testimony must carry with it the note of authority. People will not be moved by our words if they detect in what we say any hesitancy or doubt about the certainty of our own salvation. The word 'witness' after all, comes from the Greek word for martyr and means that a man is so certain of his faith in Christ that he will even die for it. We have to be able to say with Paul: 'I know whom I have believed, and am convinced that he is able to guard what I have entrusted to him for that day' (2 Timothy 1:12).

Thirdly, our witness, simply because it is based on first-hand knowledge, will have about it a certain boldness and courage. I mean this, we may not be the kind of person who finds it easy to articulate what is in our mind, or we may be of a rather timid disposition and find it difficult to communicate with others. But if the power of the Holy Spirit indwells us then we will be amazed at the courage and boldness he gives us to speak out for Christ to others. Timothy was of a rather timid and shy nature and found ministry and witness difficult but Paul reminds him that 'God did not give us a spirit of timidity, but a spirit of power, of love and of self-discipline' (2 Timothy 1:7). Like Timothy, we may need a bit of prodding to speak to other people, but once started God will honour our courage and we shall be amazed at the power and boldness which the Holy Spirit within imparts to us.

A faithful preacher of God's Word

Epaphras was a faithful, conscientious preacher and teacher of the gospel message. His ministry, to quote one writer, 'was no hit-or-miss affair with a minimum of instruction.' Rather he taught the Word of God in all its depth and fullness. That is clear from what we are told: 'this gospel is producing fruit and growing, just as it has been doing among you since the day you heard it and understood God's grace in all its truth. You learned it from Epaphras . . . who is a faithful minister of Christ' (1:6,7).

One of the greatest needs in the modern Church is for men who are able to preach and teach the Word of God in all its depth and fullness. All too often priority is given to the other things in the Church at the expense of preaching—administration, counselling, organizing events, service in the community etc. These things will have their place in the Church's function, but first and foremost the need is for the faithful exposition of the truth of God so that people's lives may be spiritually fruitful and that they may grow in their understanding of the great doctrines of Scripture. Epaphras was faithful in doing just that, whereas all too often today, even where there is preaching of a kind, the pulpit portrays a lot of woolly thinking and people drift in uncertainty and confusion.

Faithful in prayer

Epaphras had a true pastor's heart since he not only preached to people and fed their minds, but he prayed for them
ardently. His was not the two-minute 'arrow' prayer that
asks God to bless his people and congregation. Paul says:
'He is always wrestling in prayer for you' (4:12). He agon-
ized in prayer and pleaded for God's Spirit to work among
the people of the fellowship. As their shepherd he was anxious for the well-being of their souls. We are even told what
it was he wrestled for on their behalf before God: 'that you
may stand firm in all the will of God, mature and fully
assured' (v.12).

In the New Testament world there were all kinds of false
teachings, heresies and pseudo-philosophies that God's
people were prey to, and Epaphras was concerned that his
people should be sufficiently firm and mature in their salvation to resist those pressures. He hoped to do that through
faithful preaching of the Word of truth and faithful wrestling
in prayer. The same challenge faces today's pastor. Once
again there is the danger within the Church that people are
like infants, 'tossed back and forth by the waves, and blown
here and there by every wind of teaching and by the cunning
and craftiness of men in their deceitful scheming' (Ephesians
4:14). How is a pastor to guard his flock against those unset-
tling influences? Only by faithfully preaching and teaching
the Scriptures and by spending time wrestling in prayer on
their behalf.

Faithful to the local church

Being a pastor was no picnic for Epaphras. He had three
churches to care for, Colossae, Laodicea and Hierapolis, and

it would seem that he put every ounce of energy into his work. 'I vouch for him that he is working hard for you and for those at Laodicea and Hierapolis' (4:13). The work made great demands upon Epaphras spiritually, intellectually and physically and he must have been at full stretch most of the time with no intention of rusting out. The cost of it all is intimated in Philemon verse 23 where Paul speaks of him as his 'fellow-prisoner'.

God works not only through men but also through the local church, which is not so much an organization as an organism, a living dynamic company of believers knit together in bonds of fellowship and sharing a common experience of God's salvation in the Lord Jesus Christ. In the opening verses of his Epistle to the Colossians Paul refers to the believers there as 'holy and faithful brothers in Christ', thus indicating that they should see their work and witness within the framework of a family in which they seek to help one another to grow in the things of Christ and to extend the frontiers of God's kingdom in the local situation.

That is why it is such a privilege to be a member of one's local church and why we should treat it very seriously.

7
James
the Lord's brother

Read Acts 15:12-21

From the above passage we learn that James was a very important individual in New Testament times because he was the leader of the Church in Jerusalem. But his fame also lies in another direction. He was the brother of our Lord. This we learn from Paul who tells us of a visit he made to Jerusalem to discuss matters with the Apostles: 'I saw none of the other apostles—only James, the Lord's brother' (Galatians 1:19).

James—the man

We know quite a lot about James from the many references to him. It seems that, after the birth of our Lord, he was the eldest of the other children born to Mary and Joseph, since he is mentioned first in the list given by Mark: 'Isn't this Mary's son and the brother of James, Joses, Judas and Simon? Aren't his sisters here with us?' (Mark 6:3). Josephus, the Jewish historian, speaks of James's martyrdom: 'Ananus (High Priest) . . . thinking that he had a good opportunity because Festus (Governor) was dead . . . holds a judicial council and brought to it the brother of Jesus, who was called Christ—James was his name and some others on a charge of violating the Law. He gave them over to be stoned to death' (*Antiquities*, Book 20:9.i).

Eusebius in his *Ecclesiastical History* 2:23 gives a further description: 'James, he whom all from the time of our Lord to our own day call the Just . . . was holy from his mother's womb; wine and strong drink he drank not . . . no razor touched his head . . . And alone he would enter the Temple . . . so that his knees were callous like a camel's in consequence of his continual kneeling in prayer to God and beseeching pardon for the people.'

We also see from the first verse in James's Epistle that he took no special pride in the fact that he was the Lord's brother but describes himself simply as a 'servant' of the Lord Jesus Christ. Here was a man therefore, who was just and godly, a man of prayer and of a humble disposition. And yet during the earthly life of our Lord James, like other members of his family, was not a Christian believer.

James—not a believer

John gives us an interesting insight into the relationship between Jesus and his brothers: 'But when the Jewish Feast of Tabernacles was near, Jesus' brothers said to him, "You ought to leave here and go to Judea, so that your disciples may see the miracles you do. No-one who wants to become a public figure acts in secret. Since you are doing these things, show yourself to the world." For even his own brothers did not believe in him' (John 7:2,3).

Not only did James and his brothers not believe in the ministry and Messiahship of Jesus, but they treated him with an almost amused contempt. They said in effect: 'If you want to play the Messiah, don't hide in this backwater but go up to Jerusalem the capital, and show the public what you can do.' But his family actually went further and opposed the ministry of Jesus because they felt he was suffering from some kind of religious mania. Mark says: 'When his family heard about this, they went to take charge of him, for they said "He is out of his mind"' (Mark 3:21). It seems incredible to us that James and the other members of his family could have treated Christ in that way.

But it teaches us the lesson that one can get very near Christ and the things of the Spirit of God without ever crossing that line where you give your life over to him in repentance and faith. James lived in our Lord's immediate presence for years on end, saw the depth of his conduct and character and yet never came to believing faith in him as Saviour. That can still happen. You can be part of a Christian home and family, attend a Christian place of worship, even have Christian friends or move in Christian circles and yet never know Christ personally as Saviour and Lord.

Another lesson to be learned from the life of James concerns the longing many of us may have to see members of our own families being brought to faith in Christ. If Jesus had a deep compassion for the souls of men and women and saw them as 'sheep without a shepherd', then he must also have had such a love for James's soul and spiritual destiny during his earthly life. Sometimes we may be inclined to put the blame on ourselves if loved ones have not been won for Christ. We may wonder: 'Have I witnessed faithfully? Have I prayed enough? Have I set a godly example?' and so on. But that is not necessarily true. James could have had no better example than that of his brother Jesus. It all goes to show that salvation is of God. Only the Holy Spirit in convicting power can show a person that it is their sin that is keeping them from God. We must not be discouraged therefore but must keep on praying that God himself will intervene in the life of a loved one.

James's conversion

The exciting and encouraging thing about James is that he did eventually become a Christian believer, but it took the death and resurrection of the Lord Jesus to bring it about. Speaking of the resurrection appearances of Christ, Paul says this: 'He appeared to Peter, and then to the Twelve. After that he appeared to more than five hundred of the brothers at the same time . . . Then he appeared to James, then to all the apostles' (1 Corinthians 15:5-7).

What is interesting is that the risen Lord made a special appearance to James personally. Did Jesus say something like: 'James, you didn't believe in me when we were at home. Will you believe now—now that I have died and risen again to bring you into new life?' Well, whatever the actual conversation, if there was any, that is exactly what James did. He believed and entered into God's kingdom. In Acts we have a lovely picture of the whole family of Jesus, including James, meeting with the believers in prayer in readiness for the coming of the Holy Spirit. 'They all joined together constantly in prayer, along with the women and Mary the mother of Jesus, and his brothers' (Acts 1:14).

To those who are still longing for their loved ones to come to Christ, the experience of James says two things. Firstly, don't give up praying and witnessing because you don't see anything happening to them. Remember, you may never see them come to salvation in your lifetime. The Lord died and left this earthly life without James coming to faith in him. God has his own time-scale in these matters, and when it pleases him he will bring it about.

Secondly, it reminds all of us that salvation comes only through a personal experience of the risen Lord Jesus in our own life. It was only after meeting with the risen Lord that

James came to faith. But once he came into salvation his Christian life began to blossom and he went on to great things. He was used of the Holy Spirit to write part of the New Testament, the Epistle of James, and three times in the book of Acts he is mentioned as the guiding light and leader of the Church at Jerusalem. That is what God can do with any life that is given over entirely to him. Not only does he give that person the gift of eternal life, but he will bring that person's life to its full potential in his service.

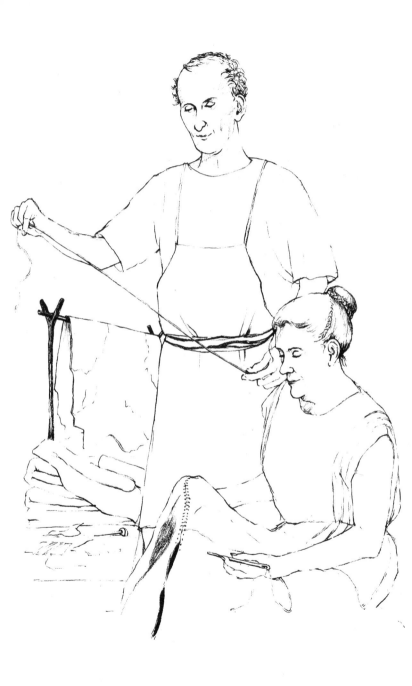

8
Aquila and Priscilla
a godly couple

Read Acts 18:1-4; 18-26

Here was a husband and wife team that is frequently mentioned in the New Testament but never separately. It seems that they were devoted to each other and were in complete harmony, not only in their marriage, but spiritually and in their desire to serve Christ.

Active Christians

It is clear that Aquila and Priscilla lived a very full and active Christian life and were the kind of couple any pastor today would be glad to have in his church. When Paul met up with them they were near enough refugees who had been forced to leave Rome because of persecution. 'After this, Paul left Athens and went to Corinth. There he met a Jew named Aquila . . . who had recently come from Italy with his wife Priscilla, because Claudius had ordered all the Jews to leave Rome' (v.1,2). How and when they became believers we are not told. But the fact that they were, together with their tent-making business, may have attracted Paul to them and they offered him the hospitality of their home as a base for his preaching operations in Corinth. 'Because he was a tentmaker as they were, he stayed and worked with them. Every

Sabbath he reasoned in the synagogue, trying to persuade Jews and Greeks' (v.3,4). This continued for eighteen months (v.11).

We next meet up with Aquila and Priscilla at Ephesus from where Paul writes to the Corinthians and refers to 'the church that meets at their house' (1 Corinthians 16:19). Then in Romans 16:3-5 we learn that they are back in Rome and once again active in the Lord's work. 'Greet Priscilla and Aquila, my fellow-workers in Christ Jesus. They risked their lives for me. Not only I but all the churches of the Gentiles are grateful to them. Greet also the church that meets at their house.'

Although they lived a strangely nomadic existence Aquila and Priscilla seemed always to be active in the Lord's work. They did not hold any special office in the church or have any special authority invested in them and yet they played such a prominent role in church life that Paul says 'all the churches of the Gentiles are grateful to them' (Romans 16:4). In that sense they represent all ordinary believers in our churches today about whom we know nothing, but without whose vital faith and hard work the life of the local church would be much the poorer.

What that is saying to us is this. God in his sovereign purpose chooses so often to work in the church through ordinary faithful unnamed believers like Priscilla and Aquila rather than through high-powered movements or organizations. Moreover, although God undoubtedly chooses special men for special tasks, like the great names of history, the ongoing day-to-day forceful advance of the kingdom of God is carried on through the prayers, witness and faithful service of countless ordinary Christians whose names will never appear in the annals of history. In that little classic *Power Through Prayer*, E. M. Bounds says this: 'The church is looking for better methods, God is looking for better men . . .

What the church needs today is not more machinery, not new organisations or more novel methods, but men whom the Holy Ghost can use—men of prayer.'

They used their home

A vital ingredient in the faith of Aquila and Priscilla was the use they made of their home in the cause of the gospel. They really did practise the exhortation of Peter to 'offer hospitality to one another without grumbling' (1 Peter 4:9) and saw their home as an extension of their Christian life. When in Corinth they allowed Paul, as we saw earlier, to make their home the base of his missionary operations for eighteen months. In verse 26 of our present chapter they welcomed Apollos into their home in order to explain the gospel more fully to him. Moreover, when they lived at Ephesus and Rome reference is made to the church at their house (1 Corinthians 16:19; Romans 16:5). Clearly they were a couple with open hearts and an open door, and their home was sanctified with the presence of God.

There is much that Christians can do to use their homes for promoting the cause of the gospel. We can invite Christian friends in for times of fellowship and prayer and the study of God's Word. We can make our homes a centre for evangelistic operations by video or to hear a tape over a cup of coffee. We can offer hospitality to visiting speakers at our local church. There are as many ways as imagination can devise for the use of our homes in furthering the work of God if we have a mind to do so.

A spirit of discernment

We are told in this chapter that Apollos preached at the synagogue at Corinth and that he was 'a learned man, with a thorough knowledge of the Scriptures' but that he 'knew only the baptism of John' (v.24,25). In other words, his preaching was defective, since he knew nothing of salvation through the saving work of Christ. Aquila and Priscilla were only two ordinary Christians, but they immediately discerned this lack of spiritual understanding in the eloquent and scholarly preacher. The result was that 'they invited him to their home and explained to him the way of God more adequately.'

The lack of spiritual discernment is a great failure in many congregations today, even in evangelical churches. As a consequence of this, all kinds of strange teachings and doctrinal aberrations are preached from our pulpits by those claiming to be ministers of the Word of God, and people accept them without discerning that they undermine and distort the authority of the Holy Scriptures. Aquila and Priscilla discerned the weakness of Apollos because they knew and loved the teaching of God's Word. Today they would be a Christian couple who pray together and who love reading and discussing God's Word as husband and wife. They were not great thinkers or theologians like Apollos, but they had an insight into the work of God's salvation that he didn't have. To them salvation was a personal reality and Christ was a personal Saviour. Theirs was not so much head knowledge as heart knowledge.

The element of daring

In his letter to the Romans Paul says something highly significant about Aquila and Priscilla—'They risked their lives for me' (Romans 16:3). What event or happening he was referring to we don't know, but clearly this couple at some time or other had been willing to lay down their lives for the cause of the gospel as reflected in Paul's ministry. Still, today in parts of the world there are believers who are having to glorify God through putting themselves in physical danger or by suffering imprisonment or even by laying down their lives.

We may not be called upon to do that, but there is still a sense in which the element of daring and risk is an ingredient of the Christian life. Do we smother our growth in discipleship by too much prudence and caution? Do we hedge ourselves around too much with the rules of 'safety first'? Faith, after all, is a willingness to venture forth, to launch out 'into the deep' or, as the hymn says: 'to dare all for Jesu's sake'. Sometimes we have to be willing to throw all caution and self-consciousness to the winds and have the courage to speak out for Christ even at the risk of being laughed at or ridiculed or ostracized because of our Christian convictions. Preaching on faith, Spurgeon said this:

> Faith is a venturesome thing and if any of you have not yet been nerved with courage, I pray that you will feel compelled to attempt more than your unaided strength can possibly do. Brethren, undertake some daring thing for Christ. Is there one who ought to preach but is too timid? I hope his faith will overcome his timidity. Is there one who ought to teach in the Sunday School but is shy and hesitant? I hope their faith will get fresh daring from their love of souls.

And let us not forget that there is such a thing as 'successful failure'. It sometimes takes great daring and courage to fail in the way that Peter did when he attempted to walk on the water to Christ. But if we fail and fall in venturing out for the Lord Jesus, he is always there to help us rise up again.

9
Festus
a sophisticated pagan

Read Acts 25:13-22

When Felix, the Roman governor mentioned in Acts 24, was recalled to Rome, he was succeeded in office by Porcius Festus before whom Paul was brought to trial following accusations brought against him by the Jewish leaders (25:1,2). Little is known about Festus from secular or scriptural sources except that he was very different from his predecessor Felix, in that his governorship was neither corrupt nor oppressive and he seems to have had a real concern for Roman justice.

Spiritual ignorance

One thing we can say for certain about Festus is that he appears to have been totally ignorant of spiritual concerns and that he did not have the slightest understanding of matters relating to God and the life of the soul. He was, as we have it in the chapter heading, a sophisticated pagan. That is clear from what he says to King Agrippa when explaining to him the trial of Paul: 'When his accusers got up to speak, they did not charge him with any of the crimes I had expected. Instead, they had some points of dispute with him about their own religion and about a dead man named Jesus whom Paul had claimed was alive. I was at a loss how to investigate such matters' (25:18-20).

Here was Paul at his trial testifying with deep sincerity to his Christian faith and the power of Christ's resurrection, and Festus says to Agrippa in effect: 'You know, I hadn't a clue what the man was on about and I am at a complete loss how to deal with him. Quite frankly, I couldn't care less about religious disputes, I'm not in the least bit interested in such things and I never even think about them. After all, I lead a very busy life running this difficult country and I have plenty of disputes and problems of my own to occupy my time.'

This abysmal ignorance of anything spiritual on the part of Festus can be seen also in his reaction to Paul's testimony: 'At this point Festus interrupted Paul's defence. "You are out of your mind, Paul!" he shouted. "Your great learning is driving you insane"' (26:24). As he saw it, Paul was suffering from some kind of religious mania, since, in his thinking, anyone who could get excited and enthusiastic about God's power to raise the dead and about matters relating to heaven and the soul must necessarily be dismissed as a crank.

In this respect, Festus represents many in our modern world. He was a cultured, intelligent man, sophisticated and urbane, but he suffered from a total inability to comprehend anything of a truly spiritual nature. There are tens of thousands like him in our own society today, and they are to be found in all walks of life. They are our neighbours, bank managers, factory workers, shop assistants, schoolteachers, doctors, computer programmers and such like. Often they are kind, intelligent, morally upright people who wouldn't dream of doing harm to anyone, but they all have one thing in common, they are totally devoid of any interest in the

things of God and of the soul, or any inclination in that direction. They feel that it is perfectly in order to get excited and
enthusiastic about sport and politics and a host of other
things, but let them see that you are excited about God and,
like Festus, they will think that you are mad.

It is as if they had no soul nor any spiritual dimension to
their being. Their whole thought and energy is centred
entirely on the physical, intellectual and material aspects of
life. They are sophisticated pagans.

Spiritual blindness

Our Lord referred directly to people like that in the Sermon
on the Mount: 'So do not worry, saying, "What shall we
eat?" or "What shall we drink?" or "What shall we wear?"
For the pagans run after all these things . . . and your heavenly
Father knows that you need them' (Matthew 6:31,32). But
what is it that makes these people so obsessed with the material, physical concerns of this life and so abysmally disinter-
ested in spiritual realities? We need to know if only because
we are meeting up with them all the time, in the places
where we work, in social relationships and in all those other
situations that bring us into contact with people. And there is
no doubt that this sophisticated kind of paganism which we
are talking about is one of the toughest, deadliest enemies of
the gospel we are up against today. Anyone who has tried to
talk to colleagues at work about the things of God, or shared
in any kind of outreach or door-to-door evangelism, will
know that this is true. As you speak to these folk about the
things of God, about repentance, forgiveness, judgment,
heaven and hell, nothing seems to penetrate. They regard
you with total disbelief and bewilderment as though you
were talking in another language. Like Festus, they simply

cannot understand or grasp why it is that anyone should be so seriously concerned with matters which, as they see it, have nothing whatever to do with real life. The terrible seriousness of their lost condition outside God means nothing whatever to them.

What is the reason for that? Well, the Bible says that such people are suffering from a spiritual blindness that blocks their minds to the perception of divine truth. 'And even if our gospel is veiled, it is veiled to those who are perishing. The god of this age has blinded the minds of unbelievers, so that they cannot see the light of the gospel of the glory of Christ who is the image of God.' (2 Corinthians 4:3,4). It is not that they 'will not' see it, but that they 'cannot' see it. Satan, the god of this age, prevents them from seeing the seriousness of their lost condition and the relevance of the gospel, and keeps them in a state of spiritual and intellectual bondage. Like Festus, such a person may have an enlightened mind about many other things and have a profound intellectual grasp of other branches of knowledge such as medicine, science, astronomy and so on, but when it comes to the things of God and the soul that person is forced to say as Festus did to Agrippa: 'I was at a loss how to investigate such matters' (25:20).

Our attitude to Festus

How are we to deal with the Festus's of this world? Is it legitimate for us to get angry and frustrated and to feel that, if such speople are too stupid or ignorant to accept the truth of the gospel when it is so clearly put to them, then we have no alternative but to wash our hands of them? We may feel that way at times but we must resist it, else we may be in danger of falling into that cynical mood of Carlyle when he described the population of England as 'thirty million, mostly fools'. We cannot give up that easily on such folk. Remember, we are not talking here about those who deliberately and calculatingly resist the truth of salvation when they clearly see and understand it. Rather we are talking about those who are oblivious to its serious import for their lives.

Our attitude should be more like that of the Lord Jesus when he saw the crowds who had come to hear him preach: 'He had compassion on them, because they were harassed and helpless, like sheep without a shepherd' (Matthew 9:36). At the spiritual level we must see people as the dupes and victims of Satan and must never be tempted to give up on them. They are not in such a hopeless condition that they cannot be delivered. The power of the Holy Spirit can open the eyes of their understanding and quicken the conscience so that the light of God's truth can dispel the darkness and bring that person to faith in Christ.

This calls for great patience on our part, especially if we have been praying for someone a long time, only to find that they remain as hard and obdurate as ever. It helps to remind ourselves that someone once bore patiently with us and did not give up praying on our behalf until eventually our hard heart was broken, the eyes of our understanding were opened and we 'saw' the truth of God's salvation in Christ. Above all, God himself was patient with us. Peter says: 'He is patient with you, not wanting anyone to perish, but everyone to come to repentance' (2 Peter 3:9). God does not delight in judging men, but he does so because that is the only thing he can do with sin. But if God, in patience, is willing to stretch the calendar before bringing men to judgment, then surely we can be patient with those we are seeking to win for Christ.

10
Agrippa
a complex personality

Read Acts 26

The story of Festus in the previous chapter is connected with that of King Agrippa and the part he played in the trial of Paul. Agrippa was totally different from Festus in many respects. To begin with he came from a Jewish background and, unlike Festus, he was both acquainted with, and deeply interested in, spiritual matters. This comes out clearly in Paul's reply to Festus when he accused him of being out of his mind: '"I am not insane, most excellent Festus," Paul replied. "What I am saying is true and reasonable. The king is familiar with these things, and I can speak freely to him. I am convinced that none of this has escaped his notice, because it was not done in a corner. King Agrippa, do you believe the prophets? I know you do."' (v.25-7).

Here then was a man who knew and understood many of the things Paul was talking about. He was not a stranger to spiritual truth but, in Paul's words, 'believed the prophets'. Yet, although he knew and believed the things of God at one level, the level of the mind, he did not believe them at the deeper level of the heart, as is evident from what we learn later.

Believing with the mind

When we dealt with the character of Felix, the Roman Governor (Acts 24), we saw that he too, like Agrippa, had an intelligent understanding of spiritual truths but it went no deeper than that.

The fact is that there has to be a certain intellectual grasp of the truths of Christianity if one is to come to real faith in the Lord Jesus Christ. When Paul came to Thessalonica we find that he entered the synagogue and 'reasoned with them from the Scriptures' (Acts 17:2). That means that he entered into debate and dialogue with the Jews and didn't simply harangue them. He appealed not only to their emotions and feelings but also to their minds and wills. His exposition of the truth of the gospel was undergirded with sound reasoning.

Some people seem to have the idea that when you become a Christian believer you have to dispense with your brains and accept everything on blind trust. That is not what faith is. On the other hand, there is an approach to the gospel which is too intellectual and in which everything has to be brought to the bar of human judgment and reason. That is 'rationalism' and it is still with us, even among church leaders and theologians who deny the supernatural and miraculous in Christianity, thereby dethroning trust in an Almighty and Sovereign God.

True faith and belief in the Lord Jesus Christ therefore involve both the mind and the heart. It is the work of the Holy Spirit to enlighten the mind in an understanding of the truths of the gospel and, at the same time, to warm the heart with the inner experience of the reality of those truths. When we speak to others of the things of God therefore, we will follow Paul's method at Thessalonica when he 'reasoned with them from the Scriptures, explaining and proving that the Christ had to suffer and rise from the dead' (Acts 17:2,3). In short, we will be rational, biblical and evangelical.

It seems that Agrippa didn't get beyond the first of these. He had an intellectual understanding of the things of God, but it went no deeper since he rejected Paul's message.

Agrippa's rejection

Whatever else we may think of Agrippa's response to Paul's testimony to his Christian faith, it is clear that the king was impressed. 'Then Agrippa said to Paul, "Do you think that in such a short time you can persuade me to be a Christian?"' (v.28). Among commentators there is a good deal of disagreement as to the meaning of Agrippa's words. The AV reads: 'Almost thou persuadest me to be a Christian.' And J. B. Phillips renders it: 'Much more of this Paul . . . and you will be making me a Christian!' Whatever emphasis we give to Agrippa's response, the fact is that he rejected the message of salvation, and that is a solemn warning to everyone.

But let us look at each of these emphases. First, there is *the serious response:* 'Almost thou persuadest me to be a Christian' (AV). He recognized the seriousness for his own soul of what Paul was saying, but he lacked the decisiveness to act upon it. He 'almost' believed. He was 'not far from the kingdom of God', as Jesus said of the teacher of the law in Mark 12:34. But to be 'not far from the Kingdom' is the same as not being in it! To be 'almost' persuaded of the truth of Christ is a poor substitute. Alexander Whyte says that '"Almost" is surely the most tragic word that is ever uttered on this earth or in hell. And yet, both earth and hell are full of it.' Why do people allow themselves to be 'almost' persuaded of the claims of Christ upon their lives but take it no further?

It may be that they fear what others may say of them if they were to commit themselves to the cause of God. Or perhaps they find the pull of the world too strong for them to leave it completely and they try to serve both God and mammon. Or possibly the cost of following Christ may be too great. They have seen what others have given up for the cause of Christ and they feel that they are not equal to it. But whatever the reason, the end is the same—they are rejecting Christ and that is a desperate situation to be in.

Secondly, it could have been *a contemptuous response:* 'Then Agrippa said to Paul, "Do you think that in such a short time you can persuade me to be a Christian?"' (NIV). We sense a note of contempt and sarcasm in a retort like that. Perhaps Agrippa resented Paul's attempt through his testimony to convert him to the Christian faith, especially in front of his pagan friend, Festus. In Agrippa's proud mind it was downright cheek for this man, a prisoner in chains, to think that he, a king and dressed as he was in all his royal magnificence (25:23), should require to be saved.

Pride is the darling sin and the greatest of all obstacles to the penetrating truth of God's Word. Pride brought about the fall of Satan from heaven where he served as Lucifer, the angel of light. Pride of intellect, pride of possessions, pride in morals, pride of position, it is all the same. It means a refusal to humble oneself in recognition of one's inner bankruptcy and spiritual poverty before the majesty and richness of God's saving grace.

Thirdly, there is *the frivolous response:* 'Much more of this Paul, and you will be making me a Christian' (J. B. Phillips). That remark tells us that Agrippa was trivializing the things of God. He didn't consider that what Paul was saying was worth taking seriously. And there are so many like that. They have a frivolous attitude towards most things. Life itself is treated as if it were something of a joke. They are light-minded, pleasure-loving people whose philosophy is 'eat, drink and be merry, for tomorrow we die.'

Of course, all this may in some cases be only a façade and the truth behind the veil may be quite different. They may be lonely, frightened people hiding from the realities of the great issues of life. But whatever their true situation, we have to urge upon these frivolous folk that they cannot trivialize God and the things of the soul without paying a heavy price. What is at stake is nothing less than their eternal destiny.

11
Barnabas
a man God could use

Read Acts 4:32-37

We place Barnabas among the lesser-known characters of the New Testament simply because he was
a fellow-missionary with Paul and therefore his
own character tends to be overshadowed by that of the great
apostle. He is introduced to us as a native of Cyprus and a
member of the tribe of Levi (v.36). He was probably a Jew of
the Diaspora or the dispersion of Jews following the Exile
when many of them settled in Cyprus and elsewhere. This
means he was a Hellenist or Greek-speaking Jew, and not a
Palestinian Jew like Peter and the other disciples.

His generosity for God

'Barnabas . . . sold a field he owned and brought the money
and put it at the apostles' feet' (v.36,37). Why is he singled
out for special mention in this way when we are told in verse
34 that others in the church did the same thing? Can it be
that, unlike the others, he held nothing back but put everything he had on the altar for God? Selling his land and giving
the proceeds to the church symbolized his total commitment
to the Lord Jesus Christ. If that is so, it tells us that Barnabas
was not a man of half-measures and for him, being a Christian, was all or nothing.

In his little booklet *True Discipleship* William McDonald
says:

> True Christianity is an all-out commitment to the Lord Jesus
> Christ. The Saviour is not looking for men and women who will
> give their spare evenings to Him—or their weekends—or their
> years of retirement. Rather He seeks those who will give Him
> first place in their lives.

Barnabas seems to have been that kind of Christian. To be
a half-hearted Christian is both insulting to the Lord we
serve and the cause of much personal misery. It means living
a divided life between the desire for an easy comfortable life-
style on the one hand, and the longing to please God by giving him more of our time, energy, money and thought on the
other. This has always been a problem for God's people. The
Psalmist said: '. . . give me an undivided heart, that I may
fear your name' (86:11). Our Lord said the same thing in
another way: 'No-one can serve two masters. Either he will
hate the one and love the other, or he will be devoted to the
one and despise the other. You cannot serve both God and
Money' (Matthew 6:24).

To be a half-hearted Christian is to be the victim of con-
flicting principles on the inside of your life, the pull of the
world and the claims of Christ. The result for many is fits of
remorse and guilt, with dissatisfaction and discontent in the
heart instead of peace and blessing. The only answer is personal discipline and a determination to take God seriously.
In the Psalm we quoted, the Psalmist prays for an undivided
heart 'that I may fear your name.' He reminds himself that
the God he serves is not to be trifled with.

An encourager

The interesting thing about Barnabas is that his original

name was Joseph but his fellow Christians changed it to Barnabas, which means Son of Encouragement (v.36). Why did they do that? Clearly, because they could see that this was a trait in his character. And we have instances of the way he encouraged others. When Saul of Tarsus tried to join the disciples at Jerusalem following his conversion, they were all very suspicious of him, because of his past:

> When he came to Jerusalem, he tried to join the disciples, but they were all afraid of him, not believing that he really was a disciple. But Barnabas took him and brought him to the apostles. He told them how Saul on his journey had seen the Lord and that the Lord had spoken to him, and how in Damascus he had preached fearlessly in the name of Jesus. So Saul stayed with them and moved about freely in Jerusalem, speaking boldly in the name of the Lord (Acts 9:26-8).

Another instance was when Gentiles began joining the church at Antioch: 'News of this reached the ears of the church at Jerusalem, and they sent Barnabas to Antioch. When he arrived and saw the evidence of the grace of God, he was glad and encouraged them all to remain true to the Lord with all their hearts (Acts 11:22,23).

It is the easiest thing in the world to be negative towards others and to be always criticizing and finding fault. In Matthew 12:20 we have a wonderful description of our Lord's ministry: 'A bruised reed he will not break, and a smouldering wick he will not snuff out . . .' That was our Lord's way of treating people of a tottering weak faith; he encouraged it back to a flame. A person's faith in seeking God's salvation may be weak and faltering and they may have all kinds of doubts and questions, but the Lord will accept that measure of faith, small though it is, and we must encourage them to put that weak faith into operation. If we look around there will always be someone in need of motivating and encouraging and we may be the very person God wants in that particular ministry.

He was used of God

In his missionary work Barnabas was greatly used of God to the conversion of others because he had the anointing of the Holy Spirit upon his life. 'He was a good man, full of the Holy Spirit and faith . . .' (Acts 11:24). We also read: 'In the church at Antioch there were prophets and teachers . . . While they were worshipping the Lord and fasting, the Holy Spirit said, "Set apart for me Barnabas and Saul for the work to which I have called them"' (Acts 13:1,2).

Often we are ineffective and powerless to win others to Christ, not because we lack motivation or desire, but because we fail to tap into the source of God's power in the Holy Spirit. The degree to which we accomplish anything in the spiritual life is determined by our openness to the power and control of the Holy Spirit in our lives. It is not our cleverness or ability to argue cogently that will win people to Christ, but the Holy Spirit working through us. When John the Baptist was asked who he was, he replied: 'I am the voice of one crying in the wilderness.' That is all the Holy Spirit needs, a voice, a willing instrument, not cleverness or eloquent speaking.

Here is a story I read that illustrates that in a wonderful way. An old chapel deacon was concerned to win for Christ the local blacksmith, who was a hard-hearted, well-read man and strong in argument. The old deacon studied as best he could, and when he felt he knew all the blacksmith's arguments, he engaged him in discussion but was easily defeated. He said tearfully, 'I can't argue with you, but I simply want you to know I have a deep concern for your soul.' Later he told his wife: 'I'm only a botch on God's work. I really do desire the salvation of the blacksmith, but in argument he laid me out cold in five minutes', and with that, he went into his room and prayed: 'O God, you know that I sincerely want to win the blacksmith for you, but I couldn't argue with him. O God, I'm only a botch on your work.' However, the blacksmith had said to his wife: 'The old deacon today brought up an argument I haven't heard before. He said he had a deep concern for my soul. What did he mean?' His wife said, 'go and ask him.' As he stood in the porch the blacksmith heard the deacon's prayer through the open window. He went inside and said: 'Deacon, you are no botch on God's work. I thought I knew all the arguments and could answer them, but you had one I have never heard before. You said you had a deep concern for my soul. Please pray for me.' And with that he trusted Christ.

That old deacon had no cogent arguments, he was just a 'voice' through whom the Holy Spirit spoke simply and compellingly.

His concern for God's glory

We saw earlier that Barnabas was sent by the apostles to supervise the work of evangelization at Antioch, because it was progressing so rapidly among the Gentiles (11:22-4). But he was unable to cope alone and sent for Saul of Tarsus to help him '. . . and when he found him he brought him to Antioch. So, for a whole year Barnabas and Saul met with the church and taught great numbers of people. The disciples were first called Christians at Antioch' (11:25,26).

In one sense that was a dangerous thing for Barnabas to have done, because he knew Saul was a man of superior gifts and that he was destined to become the great apostle to the

Gentiles and that he himself would take second place. That in fact is what happened, for from chapter 13 onwards all the emphasis in Acts is on Paul and little is said of Barnabas. But being the man he was, Barnabas didn't mind since his only concern was for the glory of God.

In the work of the gospel we all need to have an eye to the glory of God, because it serves as a wonderful antidote to any jealousy or resentment that can spring up in our hearts when we see someone else's work being more successful and more blessed of God than our own. All true success comes from God, and we can only achieve in God's work what he wants us to achieve. That was John the Baptist's reply to his disciples when they were jealous for his reputation, because of the success of Jesus' ministry. 'To this John replied, "A man can receive only what is given him from heaven"' (John 3:27). After all, whose reputation and glory do we have in mind, ours or God's?

12
Apollos
a deficient preacher

Read Acts 18:23-28

Apollos was a Jew who came from the ancient city of Alexandria which boasted one of the most famous libraries in the ancient world and had a great reputation for scholarship and learning. It was especially famous for the study of the Old Testament Scriptures. Apollos was a product of this academic environment and when he followed Paul in the preaching ministry at Ephesus he brought to it his own particular gifts of culture, refinement and eloquence.

Paul had a high estimate of him as a preacher and mentions him several times in his letters. 'What I mean is this: One of you says, "I follow Paul"; another, "I follow Apollos" . . .' (1 Corinthians 1:12). And again: 'I planted the seed, Apollos watered it, but God made it grow' (1 Corinthians 3:6).

His knowledge of the Scriptures

Here was a man who knew his Bible. 'Meanwhile a Jew named Apollos, a native of Alexandria, came to Ephesus. He was a learned man, with a thorough knowledge of the Scriptures' (v.24). That is something we should expect from a preacher, that he should be thoroughly at home with the Word of God and have the ability to explain its truth to others.

But it is not only preachers who need to know their Bible. Not all believers can expound the Word of God eloquently like Apollos, but they can benefit their own souls by reading the Scriptures regularly. Like food for the body, the Word of God does us good spiritually only when it is digested and enters our spiritual system. If Christians do not regularly read God's Word, then their souls will lack nourishment, their minds will be uninformed and their spiritual lives will be meagre and deficient.

Christians also need to be familiar with the Bible so that they can be effective in witnessing to others concerning the truth of salvation. Peter says: 'Always be prepared to give an answer to everyone who asks you to give the reason for the hope that you have' (1 Peter 3:15). He means that we should not only *be* Christians but know *why we are Christians*. We should be able to explain our faith to others. This will mean informing your mind of God's Word, knowing something of the great doctrines of the Bible—the character of God, the saving work of Christ, the person of the Holy Spirit, and so on. One doesn't have to be learned and scholarly like Apollos to know these things; they are simply the result of consistently reading God's Word.

We need to read and study the Bible also because it is a book that is meant to be lived. In it we get guidance for daily behaviour, how to spend our money, what is Christian marriage, how we should bring up our children, and so on. The Bible with its principles and commandments is meant to regulate our life in society. It is, as the Psalmist says: 'a lamp to my feet and a light for my path' (Psalm 119:105).

Zeal for God

As a preacher Apollos had a great zeal and passion for God.

'He had been instructed in the way of the Lord, and he spoke with great fervour' (v.25). We are told later: 'For he vigorously refuted the Jews in public debate, proving from the Scriptures that Jesus was the Christ' (v.28). Not all preachers have passion. Some are so flat and low-key that you get the feeling they couldn't care less whether you believe or not in what they are saying. You would never have felt that way when listening to Apollos preaching. His passion and zeal for God communicated itself to the hearers as he sought to persuade men of the truth of God.

But it is not only preachers who need to have this passion and zeal for the things of God. A Christian may be excused many things, a lack of learning and eloquence such as Apollos had, or a lack of talent or great gifts. But no believer can be excused a lack of zeal and passion for his Lord. If our hearts are not aflame with love and passion for the Saviour and for the souls of men, then there is something vital lacking in our Christian experience. We cannot fight the forces of sin and darkness with a lukewarm tepid faith. Paul tells us: 'Never be lacking in zeal, but keep your spiritual fervour, serving the Lord' (Romans 12:11).

Deficient in understanding

But with all the positive things we have said about Apollos there was something vital lacking in his understanding of the gospel, great and eloquent preacher though he was. 'He . . . taught about Jesus accurately, though he knew only the baptism of John' (v.25). He was faithful to the light he had, but it shone no further than the baptism for repentance that John had preached. And we know that John pointed beyond himself to the coming of the Lord Jesus who 'will baptize you with the Holy Spirit and with fire' (Matthew 3:11). Apollos was deficient in his understanding of salvation through the cross of Christ, the resurrection and the person and work of the Holy Spirit.

It is always a serious matter when a preacher is deficient in his understanding of salvation through the Lord Jesus Christ, since he can lead others astray, and no amount of eloquence and learning can make up for that. But it is not only preachers who need to guard against a deficient understanding of the gospel. People can labour under the deficiency of thinking that they are Christians because they go to church, or try to practise Christian values, or say their prayers, The truth is that salvation comes only through personal faith in the Lord Jesus Christ and his sacrifice on the cross for our sins. When we believe that, the Holy Spirit enters our hearts and brings us to new birth in Christ.

A teachable spirit

In the providence of God there were two people listening to Apollos that day, who suffered from no such deficiency in understanding God's salvation in Christ, and they were able to put the preacher straight. 'When Priscilla and Aquila heard him, they invited him to their home and explained to him the way of God more adequately' (v.26). Here was this great scholar and eloquent preacher showing himself quite willing to learn the way of salvation from this ordinary godly couple. It reveals him as a humble modest man with a teachable spirit, for when he moved on to Achaia he was no longer deficient in his understanding. 'For he vigorously refuted the Jews in public debate, proving from the Scriptures that Jesus was the Christ (i.e., the Messiah)' (v.28).

A teachable and humble spirit is essential if we are to know God's grace in salvation. God will do nothing for the person who has no sense of need, who is proud in spirit and who thinks they have no need of being saved. 'The sacrifices of God are a broken spirit; a broken and contrite heart, O God, you will not despise' (Psalm 51:17).

13
Simon
a spurious convert

Read Acts 8:9-25

Following the martyrdom of Stephen a wave of persecution broke out against the church in Jerusalem and the believers fled to surrounding areas. Philip went to Samaria where he preached the gospel so powerfully that many were brought to faith in Christ and others were healed of their sicknesses or delivered from evil spirits. Among those who professed faith in Christ and were baptized was Simon.

Power of the occult

This man was something of a celebrity in Samaria and had a considerable following because of his practice of sorcery. 'Now for some time a man named Simon had practised sorcery in the city and amazed all the people of Samaria. He boasted that he was someone great, and all the people, both high and low, gave him their attention and exclaimed, "This man is the divine power known as the Great Power"' (v.9,10).

Simon was no mere charlatan or trickster, as some commentators seem to suggest, but an agent of occultic forces who exercised real spiritual power. That is evident from the description given him by the people as the 'Great Power'. He was both feared and worshipped as some kind of divinity.

This was not unusual in New Testament times. In the Gospels we have many instances of our Lord casting out evil spirits and demons from people.

We might be tempted to dismiss this kind of thing as simply an ingredient in the thinking of ancient times, but that we today have progressed beyond all that. However, that would be a very foolish thing to do, since today we are experiencing in our own society something in the nature of an occult explosion, and people are again becoming enmeshed in Satanism, black magic, spiritism, witchcraft and other forms of occult practice. The reason for this may be that they are no longer satisfied with orthodox religion or formal Christianity as found in many of our churches, and therefore they are turning to these other forms of spirituality to fill the vacuum in their lives.

One thing is clear. We should never think of evil as a vague nebulous force in the universe. The Bible never speaks of evil in this way. The Lord Jesus speaks of evil as personified in the existence of Satan, a real being who is a malevolent intelligence and who plans and schemes to keep men and women in the grip and bondage of his power. And people can be set free from that bondage only by turning over their life, in faith, to the greater keeping power of God in his Son the Lord Jesus Christ. The Scriptures state categorically that 'the reason the Son of God appeared was to destroy the devil's work' (1 John 3:8). That is exactly what happened when Philip began preaching the gospel in Samaria. Satan's power exercised through the sorcery of Simon was broken and destroyed, and people entered into the joy and peace of God's forgiveness. 'But when they believed Philip as he preached the good news of the kingdom of God and the name of Jesus Christ, they were baptized, both men and women' (v.12).

It is to this same declaration of the gospel of salvation that the Church today must address itself as its most urgent task. Preachers are not there simply to give good advice, or to state their opinions on the problems of violence, crime, race-relations, and all the other evils that afflict our society. There are experts in all these areas who can do that more satisfactorily. The preacher's task, like that of Philip, is to break the power of Satan in people's lives by directing them to God's saving power in the Lord Jesus Christ.

Self-deception

Simon also serves to warn us against the danger of self-deception in the spiritual life. For we learn that under the preaching of Philip 'Simon himself believed and was baptised. And he followed Philip everywhere, astonished by the great signs and miracles he saw' (v.13). He was tremendously impressed by the things Philip did, and it was evident to him that the power of Christ was far greater than the power of his own master, Satan. On the face of it, this response of Simon was a marvellous thing, but we have to ask: Was his profession of faith genuine? This is doubtful from what we read next: 'When Simon saw that the Spirit was given at the laying on of the apostles' hands, he offered them money and said, "Give me also this ability so that everyone on whom I lay my hands may receive the Holy Spirit"' (v.18,19).

There are those commentators who maintain that Simon deliberately deceived Philip by his profession of faith in keeping with his satanic nature. For my own part, I prefer to believe that he meant it when he professed Christ and was baptized, but it didn't go deep enough. His profession of faith was at the level of the mind and not at the deeper level of the heart and spirit. He was in fact the victim of his own self-deception. He thought that he was a Christian when he wasn't. His nature had not changed. His life hitherto had been dominated by greed and a love of money, fame and power, and that was still the case since he thought that money could actually buy the power of God in the Holy Spirit. Peter's reply shows that Simon's heart was still captive to Satan: 'You have no part or share in this ministry, because your heart is not right before God . . . For I see that you are full of bitterness and captive to sin' (v.21,23).

We learn from this that people can in fact deceive themselves in thinking that they are Christians when they are not. They can make a profession of faith in the Lord Jesus Christ and be baptized in his name, and do all this sincerely, whilst at the same time they know nothing of the reality of the indwelling Holy Spirit, who brings them into newness of life.

Later, perhaps to their own amazement, they discover, like Simon, that their life has not changed on the inside. Their desires and longings are no different, and they do not experience any deep conviction of sin or a growing love for the things of God. They experience no hunger for God's Word in the Bible nor a desire for deeper communion with God in prayer. Outwardly they may appear to say and do the right things—they attend an evangelical church, use evangelical terminology, have evangelical friends and convince themselves that they are truly Christians. But they do not have the inner assurance of their salvation and from time to time this is brought home to their hearts. When it is, they should put it right before God. The seriousness of being self-deceived in this way is brought home very forcibly in a passage in Matthew's Gospel: 'Many will say to me on that day, "Lord, Lord, did we not prophesy in your name, and in your name drive out demons and perform many miracles?" Then I will tell them plainly, "I never knew you. Away from me, you evildoers!"' (7:22,23).

Clearly these people would be amazed on the judgment day to discover that they were not Christians after all. Yet they said the right things and did the right things. But the fact remains that they were self-deceived. J. C. Ryle, that wise old commentator on God's Word, says this:

> It requires far more than most people seem to think necessary to save a soul. We may be baptized in the name of Christ, boast confidently of our spiritual privileges. We may possess head knowledge and be quite satisfied with our state. We may even be preachers and teachers of others. But have we truly repented, truly believed on Christ and do we live a holy humble life? If not, then in spite of all privileges and profession we shall miss heaven at the last and be for ever cast away.

Peter urges Simon to repent (v.22), but whether he did or not we don't know. But as for ourselves we need to examine our lives closely and honestly to see if our salvation does not lie in any outward profession or in our baptism or church membership or anything else, but in the certainty of God's Spirit within our hearts.

14
Zechariah
the man God disciplined

Read Luke 1:5-25

Zechariah is not that well-known because his life tends to be overshadowed in the Gospels by that of his greater son John the Baptist. His character is worth studying however in its own right.

A godly man in a godless age

In the opening couple of verses of our passage we get a clear picture of the kind of man Zechariah was: 'In the time of Herod, king of Judea, there was a priest named Zechariah . . . his wife Elizabeth was also a descendant of Aaron. Both of them were upright in the sight of God, observing all the Lord's commandments and regulations blamelessly' (v.5,6).

This was the age of 'Herod of Judea', a godless tyrant, morally depraved and responsible for the massacre of the babies of Bethlehem at the time Christ was born. But it was a godless age in other ways. There was plenty of religion and talk about God, and Jerusalem had its temple and priesthood. But the religious scene had become in many ways ritualistic and mechanical, and it was the priests and the religious establishment who opposed the Lord Jesus and eventually brought about his death.

Nevertheless, there were exceptions, and Zechariah, with his wife Elizabeth, was one of them. They were 'upright in the sight of God, observing all the Lord's commandments'. Zechariah took his priestly calling seriously. He was not the only one to live a godly life in a godless age. There were some others who were longing for God to visit his people in the coming of the Messiah. Some are mentioned in the gospel story, like Simeon and Anna in the temple (Luke 2:25-8). Zechariah and his wife Elizabeth were part of a small godly remnant in a godless age.

We learn certain things from that. First of all, God always has his godly remnant in every age. However wicked and evil the times may be, there will always be those who remain faithful. That is true today. In a godless age like ours, when the Church is largely bankrupt, there are still fellowships where Christ is faithfully preached. There are still homes where the Bible is read and honoured as God's Word and prayer undergirds daily life. And up and down our land there are those who are praying for the soul of our nation and longing for God's Spirit to come upon us in revival power. The question is: are we among that godly remnant?

The other lesson is this: when God wants something done, he always looks for a godly person, like Zechariah, through whom he can do it. For four hundred years, since the revelation of the Old Testament, God had not spoken, and now he was about to bring in the gospel age. Who was there for him to speak to? Not the religious leaders who had become so cold and formal. He chose an elderly devout couple— Zechariah and Elizabeth. We might think that the important people for the future of our nation today are the clever, dynamic, get-up-and-go kind of people, the young ambitious people in politics, sport, commercial life and the mass-media. Well, they have their place, but God is concerned about the moral and spiritual life of our nation and he wants godly people through whom to work, whether they are young or old, clever or otherwise.

The angel of the Lord

'Then an angel of the Lord appeared to him, standing at the right side of the altar of incense' (v.11). Talk about angels and some people get distinctly uncomfortable. But the Bible has a lot to say about them. This angel told Zechariah his name—Gabriel (v.19), and that his function was to wait in God's presence until he received orders for his next errand to earth. It was Gabriel who announced to Mary the birth of Jesus (v.26). Seven centuries before he had appeared to Daniel with a message from God (Daniel 8:16). What are we to make of all this? To my mind believing in angels is no more difficult than believing in the presence of the risen Lord Jesus.

What is interesting and exciting is something our Lord said about ourselves and the angels. 'At the resurrection people will neither marry nor be given in marriage; they will be like the angels in heaven' (Matthew 22:30). We shall be like the angels in beauty and strength with bodies no longer subject to disease or pain or death. And we shall be perfect like the angels in purity and holiness, without sin and no longer having to struggle with the awful moral dilemmas that face us in this life. That is the glorious prospect for all who love the Lord Jesus Christ.

Zechariah's fear

How would we react, I wonder, if we were suddenly confronted by an angel of God? We can understand the response of Zechariah when we are told: '. . . he was startled and was gripped with fear' (v.12). But it was not a craven fear. Rather

it was a godly fear, a sense of awesome reverence that gripped him when he realized that he was in the presence of the
holy God.

The author of Hebrews says; 'Let us . . . worship God
acceptably with reverence and awe, for our God is a consum-
ing fire' (12:28,29). Is that how we worship God? Do we
come into his presence, whether in a church service or in our
personal devotions, with a deep hush upon our souls, with
the abasement of all pride and the recognition of God's holiness and our own unworthiness? For there is a tendency
today to adopt a very laid-back attitude towards the worship
of God. There is a forgetfulness of his transcendence and
'otherness' and we may approach him as if we were on equal
terms. But we are not on equal terms. Let us never forget that
he is the Creator and we are the creatures of his making.

Delayed answers to prayer

For all his contentment and godliness Zechariah nevertheless had one great heartache—he was childless. He and
Elizabeth had prayed for years about this, but now 'they
were both well on in years' (v.7) and had probably given up
praying and accepted the fact that God didn't want them to
have a child. But now suddenly here was the angel saying:
'Do not be afraid, Zechariah; your prayer has been heard.
Your wife Elizabeth will bear you a son, and you are to give
him the name John.' And then there follows a wonderful
description of the kind of son he would be. So God heard the
prayer after all and here was the answer years later.

We all have our burdens and heartaches, and when we
pray about them we can rest assured that God does hear, and
even if the answer doesn't come immediately, he has not forgotten us. That wise old commentator Matthew Henry says:

'God files our prayers in heaven though the answer is not presently given us.' I don't know why God doesn't answer immediately, but he must have his reasons which we don't know about. Unless God gives a definite negative in response to our prayers the best rule is to keep on praying and wait patiently for God's own time.

Zechariah's unbelief

It comes as a disappointment to learn that after all the years he had been praying for a child, when the answer finally came Zechariah did not believe it. 'Zechariah asked the angel, "How can I be sure of this? I am an old man and my wife is well on in years." The angel answered . . . "And now you will be silent and not able to speak until the day this happens, because you did not believe my words . . ."' (v.18,20).

His refusal to believe was inexcusable because the evidence was so clear. Standing before him was God's messenger straight from the heavenly throne. What more could he want? Zechariah was a man of faith and godliness and yet at the crucial point his faith failed. God gives us clear promises and directions in his Word and we don't believe him. In spite of our profession of faith we act sometimes as if he doesn't exist or has never spoken.

The same is true of the non-Christian. Paul says: '. . . what may be known about God is plain to them . . . his eternal power and divine nature have been clearly seen, being understood from what has been made, so that men are without excuse' (Romans 1:19,20). Every day man enjoys the evidence of God's presence and power in the miracles of creation and yet he refuses to believe. He is without excuse and God in his righteous anger says he will bring man to Judgment.

In essence, Zechariah's disappointing response was a refusal to believe that God is God. Because he and Elizabeth were old he couldn't accept that it was possible for them to have a child. Had he forgotten Abraham and Sarah? Worse still, had he forgotten that God is God? Nothing is impossible with God. The angel said to Abraham, 'Is anything too hard for the Lord?'

When our faith falters and doubt creeps in we must be careful to let God be God and remind ourselves that nothing is too hard for the Lord.

15
Ananias and Sapphira
a couple of cheats

Read Acts 5:1-10

When we considered the characters of Aquila and Priscilla we said that they were a godly couple any pastor would be glad to have in his church. The husband and wife we are now considering, Ananias and Sapphira, were very different and a definite hindrance to the work of the Church. Indeed they appear in the story of the infant Church as a warning to us not to treat our place in the Christian fellowship lightly. For here were two people who claimed to be part of God's people and yet set themselves deliberately to lie to the Holy Spirit and to cheat on God. For that they paid a heavy price in coming under God's judgment and in forfeiting their lives.

The Church a mixed company

If we look at the background to the story of Ananias and Sapphira (Acts 4:32-6) we shall see that the Church on earth is always a mixed company and therefore very imperfect. Here we have the picture of the early believers exhibiting a real sense of spiritual unity in the Lord and giving practical expression to their concern for each other's material welfare so that no one was in need. 'For from time to time those who owned lands or houses sold them, brought the money from the sales and put it at the apostles' feet, and it was distributed to anyone as he had need' (4:34,35). That kind of practical concern must always characterize the Church today. In our local fellowships there should be a desire to help one another materially and physically as well as at the spiritual level. Paul reminds us of this: 'Therefore, as we have opportunity, let us do good to all people, especially to those who belong to the family of believers' (Galatians 6:10). John says the same: 'If anyone has material possessions and sees his brother in need but has no pity on him, how can the love of God be in him?' (1 John 3:17).

In this presentation of the church at Jerusalem as a happy united family we are then given a concrete example of this sharing caring attitude in Barnabas. 'Joseph . . . called Barnabas . . . sold a field he owned and brought the money and put it at the apostles' feet' (4:36). On the face of it all is sweetness and light, but then this picture of the Christian fellowship, as an instance of true spirituality in the midst of the dishonesty and viciousness of the pagan world of that time, is totally spoiled by Ananias and Sapphira acting in such a hypocritical and dishonest manner as to bring down God's judgment in a terrible way.

But that is how the visible Church on earth is—a mixed company of people having its Barnabas's and Aquilas and Priscillas but also its Ananias's and Sapphiras. It is made up of both wheat and tares. And the Bible never hides that unpleasant fact from us because it is concerned only with the truth. The Bible never fantasizes or sentimentalizes about human nature, not even in the Church. Within the Christian community there is corruption, hypocrisy, lying and cheating as in the world, and in the final analysis it is only God who knows who are truly his within the Church.

That says two things to us. It reminds us that we come to God's house and share in its worship services, not because it is the respectable thing to do or because we have illusions about ourselves that those in the Church are better than other folk. No, we go to God's house because we are conscious of our weakness and sin and because of our desperate need to know more of God's saving grace in our lives. It is precisely because we are sinful and imperfect that we come to worship God and seek his forgiveness.

It reminds us also that our salvation does not depend upon being part of the visible organized Church here on earth. Ananias and Sapphira were part of the early fellowship of believers but God nevertheless brought a terrible judgment upon them. We can be part of a church's life and worship, sing in the choir, hold office, even that of minister or pastor, participate in the sacraments and in general share in all that is holy and sacred and yet, at the same time, be far from God, knowing nothing whatever of salvation through the work of the Holy Spirit in our hearts. We must therefore be clear in our own minds where salvation lies. It is not in church membership or baptism or anything else but through repentance and personal faith in Christ alone. Failing this we shall fall under the judgment of God at the last as surely as Ananias and Sapphira did.

Cheating God

What exactly was the sin for which Ananias and his wife both paid with their lives? 'When Ananias heard this, he fell down and died' (v.5). 'At that moment she fell down at his feet and died' (v.10). It was not that they refused to give to God's cause in the way that other members of the fellowship had done. '. . . he kept back part of the money for himself, but brought the rest and put it at the apostles' feet' (v.2). They were not guilty of selfishness therefore. Nor was it sinful to keep for themselves part of the money they received for the property they had sold. After all it was rightfully their money and they could do as they liked with it. Even Peter says that: 'Didn't it belong to you before it was sold? And after it was sold, wasn't the money at your disposal?' (v.4).

Their sin lay in the fact that they cheated on God. They deliberately conspired together to deceive God. 'With his wife's full knowledge he kept back part of the money for himself' (v.2). They lied to the Holy Spirit. 'Then Peter said, 'Ananias, how is it that Satan has so filled your heart that you have lied to the Holy Spirit and kept for yourself some of the money you received for the land?' (v.3). They mocked God and showed contempt for God by claiming that the money they were giving to his Church was the whole amount when in fact it was only a part. That is why the judgment of God fell so heavily on them, because they treated him as if he didn't matter. That is the ultimate blasphemy, to treat God as though he doesn't count and to think of sin as trivial because God will never know about it. It is an insult where God is concerned, because it is saying that he is indifferent to evil and moral wrongdoing in the world.

That is the mistake that modern man makes all the time. He lives and acts as if God wasn't there or, if he is there, he is not wise enough or intelligent enough to know what is happening here below. Therefore man wallows in his spiritual pollution in the mistaken idea that he can hide it from God or that God is ignorant of it all. But he is wrong on both counts. The Bible is consistent in its teaching that one of God's greatest attributes is his omniscience, that he sees and knows everything. The Psalmist spells it out clearly: 'O Lord, you have searched me and you know me. You know when I sit and when I rise: you perceive my thoughts from afar. You discern my going out and my lying down; you are familiar with all my ways. Before a word is on my tongue you know it completely, O Lord' (Psalm 139:1-4).

A frightening and encouraging truth

It is both a frightening and an encouraging truth that God knows and sees everything that goes on here below. It all depends on our relationship with God.

It is frightening if we have anything to hide from God because we shall all be accountable on the day of judgment for the life we live here and now, and all the hidden things will then be revealed. The time to expose them and receive God's forgiveness therefore is now. 'Nothing in all creation is hidden from God's sight. Everything is uncovered and laid bare before the eyes of him to whom we must give account' (Heb. 4:13).

For the believer it is a comforting thought that God knows and sees everything because it means that God knows all about us personally and individually. He knows our inner troubles and heartaches and the things we cannot share with others. He knows our inner aspirations and longings after holiness. In the Lord Jesus Christ he has made our life his life and has entered into all our human experiences, even our sinfulness, by taking our sins upon himself on the cross of Calvary. So although there are ugly things, hidden from others, in the 'polluted chambers' of our hearts which are clearly known to God, we have the comfort of knowing that these too are covered by the holiness and righteousness of Christ our Saviour.

16
Herod
the man with a guilty conscience

Read Mark 6:14-29

There are three Herods mentioned in the Gospels, and the one we are now considering was Herod Antipas, son of Herod the Great, who reigned during the time of our Lord's birth and was responsible for the massacre of the innocents at Bethlehem. What do we know of the character of Herod Antipas?

Well, our Lord described him as 'that fox' (Luke 13:32), which was hardly a compliment, and suggests that he was crafty, cunning and full of intrigue and treachery. This is in fact borne out by the Jewish historian Josephus, who was a contemporary, and who describes him as 'cruel, scheming, vacillating and utterly evil', and then goes on to talk of his licentiousness, his extravagant life-style, and finally his fall from power and banishment from his kingdom. In our present passage we see all these evil characteristics revealing themselves in the wicked murder of John the Baptist.

A troubled conscience

'King Herod heard about this, for Jesus' name had become well known. Some were saying, "John the Baptist has been raised from the dead . . ." Others said, "He is Elijah." . . . But when Herod heard this, he said, "John, the man I beheaded, has been raised from the dead!"' (v.14-16). Herod heard of the miracles and healings Jesus was carrying out and the rumours about who this remarkable person might be. Immediately his guilty conscience reminds him of his wickedness in putting a godly man like John the Baptist to death. He was thoroughly frightened, and thought that John had come back from the dead to seek vengeance on him. It is a terrible thing to live with a guilty conscience.

The Bible has a lot to say about conscience. We all have one; it is a part of the moral equipment God gives us at our birth. However fallen and corrupt a man is, there is this inner witness of conscience which gives a measure of light to live by. Paul says that those who have never heard the gospel will be judged according to the light of conscience, '. . . their consciences also bearing witness, and their thoughts now accusing, now even defending them. This will take place on the day when God will judge men's secrets through Jesus Christ . . .' (Romans 2:15,16).

Conscience of itself however is not sufficient to make us lead a godly life. Its sensitivity to sin and wrongdoing can be deadened so that it is no longer a reliable guide for behaviour. In the way that dust can interfere with the delicate mechanism of a fine watch, so there are all sorts of things that can interfere with the workings of conscience. Bad company, the influence of certain books we read, the films and television programmes we watch, can all upset the balance of conscience. Just as a fine watch has to be cleaned and maintained to help it to work properly in telling the time, so conscience has to be kept in good repair if it is to be a reliable guide. Just as a watchmaker maintains a watch, so God our Maker, by his Spirit within us, keeps our conscience, and has it accuse us and fill us with a sense of deep guilt, as happened in the case of Herod.

Resisting the Holy Spirit

The strange thing about Herod was that he both disliked John the Baptist and yet respected him at the same time. 'Herod feared John and protected him, knowing him to be a righteous and holy man. When Herod heard John, he was greatly puzzled; yet he liked to listen to him' (v.20).

Although Herod had imprisoned John, it is probable that he would never have put him to death had it not been for his wife, Herodias. She hated John because he publicly condemned her adulterous marriage to Herod and she was determined to bring about his death (v.17-19). Herod liked to hear John preach, but when he did so he was 'greatly puzzled'. That means he was perplexed and disturbed in his heart, not knowing how to respond to God's Word. On the one hand, he knew John was right when he spoke of the righteousness of God, and felt condemned because of his cruelty, greed and licentiousness, but at the same time he was unable to bring himself to repent.

In this way, God by the Holy Spirit was convicting Herod and giving him an opportunity to straighten out his life, but he persisted in resisting the Spirit. That still happens. A person can hear the preaching of the gospel of salvation and, in the disturbance and perplexity it brings to their mind and soul, they know that God is speaking to them of the need to repent. And yet, like Herod, they resist the Spirit and never get to the point of finding peace with God. The solemn thing is that the more one resists the harder the heart becomes, so that eventually one is incapable of responding at all.

A weak man

Herod, in spite of his outward pomp and arrogant life-style, was essentially a weak man. This comes out in the following passage: 'On his birthday Herod gave a banquet for his high officials and military commanders and the leading men of Galilee. When the daughter of Herodias came in and danced, she pleased Herod and his dinner guests. The king said to the girl, "Ask me for anything you want, and I'll give it to you." . . . She went out and said to her mother, "What shall I ask for?" "The head of John the Baptist", she answered . . . The king was greatly distressed, but, because of his oaths and his dinner guests, he did not want to refuse her. So he immediately sent an executioner with orders to bring John's head' (v.21-6).

Herod's weakness of character is seen there in three ways. He was easily influenced by others. Herodias had already pressurized him into imprisoning John and now she got him to consent to John's death. He was dominated by his own passions. Salome (as she was called) would have danced in the licentious manner that characterized high society at that time and it was calculated to stir the animal passions in Herod. Then he was a victim of pride. Having made his drunken boast to give Salome anything she asked, he did not have the moral strength to climb down and lose face in front of his dinner guests. As a king he presents us with a pathetic figure of weakness.

We can learn from that, because we also can be weak at times. We can be easily pressurized and influenced by others if we are not careful. Paul says: 'Don't let the world around you squeeze you into its own mold' (Romans 12:2—J. B. Phillips). It can easily happen. At work, school or college we can allow the godlessness and materialism of the age to squeeze and pressure us into its own mold of thinking and behaving. And our own pride and passions can also dominate and govern our lives if we do not keep a firm grip on them. To resist these pressures we need the inner strength that God's Spirit imparts through regular prayer, the reading of God's Word, the fellowship of God's people and the discipline of worship.

Rejected by Christ

The most fearful thing concerning Herod is the fact that ultimately God had nothing more to say to him. In Luke's account of the trial of Jesus we learn that he was brought before Herod: 'When Herod saw Jesus, he was greatly pleased, because for a long time he had been wanting to see him . . . he hoped to see him perform some miracle. He plied him with many questions, but Jesus gave him no answer . . . Then Herod and his soldiers ridiculed and mocked him' (Luke 23:8-11).

As the years passed Herod's heart had grown harder and harder towards the things of God. Confronted by Jesus all he wanted was to be entertained and have some new thrill. He refused to take Jesus seriously and treated Him with ridicule and contempt. But our Lord's refusal to answer Herod's questions is full of solemn implications. Was it a judicial silence; the silence of judgment upon Herod? Had Herod forfeited his claim upon the salvation of God?

That is a fearful possibility for anyone who continually resists the working of God's Spirit and refuses to take Christ and his gospel seriously. Isn't that what our Lord had in mind when he said: 'But whoever blasphemes against the Holy Spirit will never be forgiven; he is guilty of an eternal sin' (Mark 3:29). That man or woman who, like Herod, persistently rejects God's offer of salvation may yet find a day coming when they will call upon God and he will refuse to answer.

17
Stephen
the first Christian martyr

Read Acts 6 and 7

We learn from chapter six that, as the church at Jerusalem began to grow, it encountered certain problems with regard to its organization and administration. One of these problems concerned the distribution of social relief to its members. '. . . when the number of disciples was increasing, the Grecian Jews . . . complained against the Hebraic Jews, because their widows were being overlooked in the daily distribution of food' (v.1). To overcome this difficulty, the Apostles introduced the first officers in the church's organization to administer this social relief, whilst they concentrated their efforts on the spiritual leadership of the church (v.2-4). Of the seven men chosen for this task, Stephen's name heads the list (v.5).

His character

What kind of man was Stephen? His name in Greek, Stephanos, means 'crown', which was appropriate in his case, since he did in fact crown his life's work of witness with martyrdom, for which he received the 'crown of righteousness' at the hand of God (2 Timothy 4:8). Clearly, he was a man of gifts and ability, especially the gift of preaching and teaching the Word of God, which we gather from verses 9-10:

93

'Opposition arose, however . . . These men began to argue with Stephen, but they could not stand up against his wisdom or the Spirit by which he spoke.' But more important than his natural talents was his godliness and spirituality, which led his fellow church members to choose him for office in the first place: 'This proposal pleased the whole group. They chose Stephen, a man full of faith and of the Holy Spirit . . .' (v.5). And again: 'Now Stephen, a man full of God's grace and power, did great wonders and miraculous signs among the people'(v.8).

We may not have Stephen's natural gifts and talents, but all of us can emulate him in his godliness and spirituality. No one has a monopoly of the Holy Spirit and of God's grace, not even the Stephens of the Church. Holiness is not something with which we are born, it is something to be pursued in the Christian life, regardless of whether or not we are gifted and intelligent as Stephen was. Godliness and sanctity is something which the Holy Spirit creates in us as our lives are opened to his influence. As the hymn says:

> *'Tis thine to cleanse the heart,*
> *To sanctify the soul,*
> *To pour fresh life in every part,*
> *And new create the whole.*

There are two things we can keep in mind about this whole question of holiness and sanctity. Firstly, we must not run away with the idea that it has something to do with our personal psychological make-up. By that I mean the idea that some people have the kind of temperament whereby they are of a naturally contemplative and thoughtful disposition, which makes it easier to open themselves to godly influences. That is not so. Peter says: 'His divine power has given us everything we need for life and godliness through our knowledge of him who has called us by his own glory and goodness' (2 Peter 1:3). That means that Stephen had no more of the Holy Spirit than we need for the life of godliness, simply that he made better use of the Spirit's power. Holiness and sanctity have nothing whatever to do with temperament or natural disposition and everything to do with whether or not we really desire it.

Then, secondly, we are told something quite remarkable about Stephen in verse 15: 'All who were sitting in the Sanhedrin looked intently at Stephen, and they saw that his face was like the face of an angel.' Whatever that means it is certainly saying that the features of Stephen reflected the glory and holiness of God in the way that the face of Moses shone with the glory of God when he came down from Mount Sinai after receiving the commandments (Exodus 34:29). The lesson for us surely is that we all reflect in some way the light of the things that we live by. If we live life at the level of the cheap superficial values of this world, then our characters will reflect that kind of outlook. Likewise, if we live in the light of the truth and holiness of the gospel, then we are bound to reflect something of the glory of God in the face of Jesus Christ.

He began humbly

Stephen did not assume a prominent leadership role in the preaching and teaching ministry of the Church right from the outset. That only came later. He began his service for God in the much humbler role of those whose job it was to 'wait on tables' (v.2). It was as the Church began to grow (v.7) that his gifts became increasingly recognized, and his area of ministry expanded into the work of evangelizing. He started low and went up higher.

All that is in keeping with the teaching of the Lord Jesus in the parable of the talents: 'Well done, good and faithful servant! You have been faithful with a few things; I will put you in charge of many things' (Matthew 25:21). If we want God to honour our work and witness with greater blessing and greater opportunities for service, then we must first prove ourselves faithful in the little things of life and in the small opportunities that come to us. The trouble with some is that they want to begin as an 'up front' person in the work of their local church before proving themselves in the lower ranks of service. Stephen teaches us to begin low if we want to be called higher in God's service.

He was familiar with God's Word

We cannot help but be impressed with the able way Stephen handled himself in theological debate with those who opposed his message: 'These men began to argue with Stephen, but they could not stand up against his wisdom or the Spirit by which he spoke' (v.9,10). And the whole of chapter seven is given to Stephen's defence before the Sanhedrin which consists of God's dealings with his people in Old Testament history. It all speaks eloquently of his familiarity with the Scriptures.

When earlier we looked at the character of Apollos we saw that he too had a 'thorough knowledge of the Scriptures' (Acts 18:24). We said then, and we repeat it now in relation to Stephen, that if we want our witness to be effective in telling others of God's salvation, then we need to know our Bible. We do not all have Stephen's ability, but the most ordinary Christians can read God's Word and become familiar with it. This will not only equip us for witness, but without it our souls will lack nourishment and our spiritual life will be deficient.

Where the non-Christian is concerned, Stephen's remarks to those who opposed God's Word are deeply significant: 'You stiff-necked people . . . You always resist the Holy Spirit'. Indeed, so serious is it that Jesus said it can never be forgiven: 'But whoever blasphemes against the Holy Spirit will never be forgiven; he is guilty of an eternal sin' (Mark 3:29). The person who wilfully and persistently rejects the truth of God's Word is placing himself in danger of committing this eternal sin through hardening his own heart to the point where he is unable to receive God's forgiveness. We need to remind people of this when witnessing to them.

How he died

Stephen died as he had lived, with the absolute certainty in his heart of the existence of that eternal world into which he was about to enter: 'But Stephen, full of the Holy Spirit, looked up to heaven and saw the glory of God, and Jesus standing at the right hand of God. "Look", he said, "I see heaven open and the Son of Man standing at the right hand of God"' (7:55,56). With those words on his lips, he was stoned to death. But it is significant that no one else present had that vision of the reality of God and the eternal world, only Stephen. His accusers didn't have it because they were spiritually blind to such realities. They were among those of whom Paul said: 'The god of this age has blinded the minds of unbelievers, so that they cannot see the light of the gospel of the glory of Christ . . .' (2 Corinthians 4:4). The certainty of heaven and of the eternal world is only for those whose hope is in God and whose faith for salvation is centred in the Lord Jesus Christ.

18
Joseph
the secret disciple

Read Luke 23:50-56

Joseph of Arimathea was a somewhat mysterious individual. We know nothing of him prior to the crucifixion of our Lord and then only in connection with the burial. However, the incident is recorded in all four Gospels and that is what gives it significance. Perhaps his very mysteriousness is why so many legends have grown up around Joseph, including the one about his coming to Glastonbury, where he stuck his staff into the ground, and it became the Glastonbury thorn.

But what about the facts? According to the four Gospels:

- he was a member of the Jewish Council or Sanhedrin.
- he did not consent to the condemnation of Jesus.
- he was a godly man, waiting for the coming of God's kingdom.
- he was a rich man.
- he went to Pilate and claimed the body of Jesus, and gave it a decent burial in his own unused tomb.
- he was a secret disciple.

Fulfilled prophecy

By his love and compassion for the Saviour in his death, Joseph helped to fulfil a prophecy concerning the Messiah given centuries before. When our Lord spoke his final words on the cross . . . 'It is finished', the work of sacrifice for sins was accomplished. All was now over and the crowd drifted away. The next step would have been that the bodies of the two thieves would have been taken down and thrown into the common grave, or else left for the vultures and scavenger dogs. The same would have happened to the body of Jesus, had not Joseph appeared on the scene: 'As evening approached there came a rich man from Arimathea, named Joseph . . . [he] took the body, wrapped it in a clean linen cloth, and placed it in his own new tomb that he had cut out of the rock' (Matthew 27:57,59).

What is significant about Joseph's act is that it was foretold some eight centuries before by the prophet Isaiah. 'He was assigned a grave with the wicked and with the rich in his death' (53:9). The intention of the Jewish authorities would have been to assign a common grave, along with the two thieves (the wicked), for the body of the Lord Jesus. But God had another assignment for the body of his Son. At the crucial moment, this rich man Joseph came forward to claim the body of our Lord, and gave it a decent burial in his own garden tomb.

There are two things we can learn from this. Firstly, it confirms the validity of the Bible as the Word of God. Here was a prophecy fulfilled centuries after it was first pronounced, and therefore those prophecies which relate to the future will also be fulfilled in the plan and purpose of God. That is a sober thought for the non-Christian, because the New Testament prophesies that the Lord Jesus is going to return to this world to sum up human history, to judge the living and the dead, to bring about the destruction of creation, and usher in the 'new heaven and the new earth' which will be inhabited only by those who acknowledge him as Saviour and Lord (2 Peter 3:10).

Also, it tells us that God always has a man in the right place at the right time to fulfil his purpose. We hear nothing of Joseph before the crucifixion and it seems as though God was reserving his part in the gospel story for this crucial moment. He would not have known that he was fulfilling prophecy when he claimed the body of Jesus and buried it in the garden tomb he was rich enough to own. But that in fact is what he was doing and he was furthering the purpose of Almighty God.

We who love God can also have our crucial moments in which we further the purpose of God in the world. It may only be a small thing we are called to do, a small part to play perhaps in the total ministry of the church. But it will have its own significance in the overall plan and purpose of God, and so we must treat it seriously whatever it is: teaching children, leading young people, stewarding at a service, preaching a sermon, leading the music, or whatever. Jesus said that even giving a cup of cold water has its place in God's scheme of things (Mark 9:41).

Secret Discipleship

In John's account of Joseph we are told that prior to the crucifixion he was a secret follower of Christ: 'Now Joseph was a disciple of Jesus, but secretly because he feared the Jews' (19:38).

Joseph had a faith, but it was a hidden faith. He loved the Lord Jesus, accepted the truth of his gospel, believed it was needed in the world, but kept it all a secret. And John tells us why—'because he feared the Jews.' He was afraid of what others might think of him, especially his fellow-members on the prestigious Jewish Council. He couldn't face the sneers and contempt if they found out that he was a follower of the very one they wanted to put to death. Luke says that he 'had not consented to their decision and action' (23:51). That is, he didn't speak against Jesus, but he didn't speak up for him either! Perhaps he feared for his wealth and comfortable lifestyle. Whatever the reason, Joseph kept his faith in the dark, and that is something to be warned against.

Are we secretive about our Christian discipleship? Is it something we are reticent about, and never like to talk about? If so, why? Is it because, like Joseph, we fear the sneers and ridicule of others? It all comes down to this in the end—how deep is our faith in the Lord Jesus Christ? Do we love Christ totally and absolutely? Does he mean more to us than the opinions of other people?

There are at least three scriptural reasons why we should not be afraid to publicize our Christian convictions. What progress would ever have been made in the work of the Church if all Christians through the ages had kept their faith a secret? We ourselves would not be in the Church, because the Christian faith would long since have been extinguished. 'Go into all the world and preach the good news . . .' (Mark 16:15). Then, do we realize how we hurt and grieve God's Spirit when we are ashamed to publicly own Christ as Saviour and Lord? Paul says, 'And do not grieve the Holy Spirit of God, with whom you were sealed for the day of redemption' (Ephesians 4:30). And yet, it is that very redemption we are ashamed of when we keep our faith hidden. Most serious of all, what if Christ is ashamed of us? This is what he said: 'If anyone is ashamed of me and my words in this adulterous and sinful generation, the Son of Man will be ashamed of him when he comes in his Father's glory with the holy angels' (Mark 8:38). What a solemn word! Far better to own him now, whatever others may think, than to be disowned by him on the Judgment Day.

Bold for Jesus

But Joseph didn't keep his discipleship a secret for ever. Mark says: 'Joseph of Arimathea . . . went boldly to Pilate and asked for Jesus' body' (15:43). That word 'boldly' tells us that it took great courage to confront Pilate in that way and openly identify with Christ. It was Joseph's way of throwing off the cloak of secrecy and let it be known that he belonged to Christ. He didn't care now what his fellow councillors, or anyone else for that matter, thought of him. Like Paul later he could now say: 'I am not ashamed of the gospel, because it is the power of God for the salvation of everyone who believes' (Romans 1:16).

What was it that changed Joseph from a frightened rabbit into a bold lion? It must have been the power of the cross of Jesus. Prior to the crucifixion he had heard our Lord speak and had witnessed his miracles and healings, but none of these things had brought his faith out into the open. But having seen our Lord on the cross dying for man's sin, including his own, he could be ashamed no longer. The truth is that when we allow that greatest of all truths, the substitutionary death of Christ for our sins, to grip our minds and sink down into our hearts, then all else falls into perspective. What others think of us, the world's way of doing things, popularity and pride all seem so trivial by comparison with what he has done in rescuing us from the dominion of darkness and in bringing us into God's kingdom of love and righteousness. We cannot help but make it known.

> *His only righteousness I show,*
> *His saving truth proclaim;*
> *'Tis all my business here below*
> *To cry, 'Behold the Lamb!'*

19
Silas
the man in the shadows

Read Acts 15:22-41

In this passage Silas is mentioned four times. In verse 12 he is described as a church leader; in verse 27 as an emissary of the church, and in verse 32 he is called a prophet. In verse 40 he is Paul's travelling companion. He is also mentioned a dozen times or more elsewhere in the New Testament. Yet for all that, he is not a well-known character. Like Paul he was both a Jew and a Roman citizen, and these were great assets as he travelled on missionary work throughout the Empire. He was also closely associated with the Apostle Peter.

Content with second place

We said when looking at the life of Barnabas that his own part in the work of the Church was overshadowed by that of the apostle Paul. The same was true, but to an even greater extent, of Silas. He was himself a gifted and intelligent man, as we shall see shortly. But he was quite content to work in the shadow of the two great apostles, Peter and Paul. For years he accompanied Paul on his missionary travels and shared in the many hardships and trials that the apostle went through. But whereas Paul's part in the work of evangelization is dealt with in great detail, Silas is given only a passing mention. The same is true of his association with Peter. We have an example of that in Peter's own words: 'With the help of Silas, whom I regard as a faithful brother, I have written to you briefly . . .' (1 Peter 5:12).

That is a very important statement, because Bible scholars tell us that Peter's Epistle is written in a highly polished, cultivated, literary Greek, which Peter, a fisherman, would hardly have used. Silas, on the other hand, as a highly gifted man and a Roman citizen, may well have taken down the contents of the letter from Peter, and was responsible for giving it its final literary shape. Hence Peter's comment: 'With the help of Silas . . . I have written to you . . .' Silas, however, was quite content to have his own gifts eclipsed as long as God was honoured.

John the Baptist showed a similar willingness to take the lower place when he said of Jesus: 'He must become greater; I must become less' (John 3:30). It takes a 'big' man to be willing to live in the greatness of others when he has so much to give himself. Silas could easily have been an 'up-front' man in every sense of the word since he had the gifts and qualities, as we shall see shortly. But in Christian work we must be willing to remain in the background and in the shadows as long as the gospel goes forward and God is glorified. Isn't that what Paul had in mind when he said: 'But we have this treasure in jars of clay to show that this all-surpassing power is from God and not from us' (2 Corinthians 4:7).

A gifted leader

Silas, as we have indicated, was in his own right a gifted leader whose qualities were quickly recognized by the church. When it came to choosing a delegation to undertake a sensitive mission in making known to the churches the decision of the Council of Jerusalem, the apostles and elders chose Silas and Judas Barsabbas, 'two men who were leaders among the brothers' (v.22).

There is today a crisis in world leadership. On the whole the political leadership shown by Western governments is of poor quality, as is evident from the stories of scandal and corruption in high places which make the news so frequently. When it comes to God's work in the local church, it is even more important that those with the right gifts and qualities are put in the leadership rôle. As the church expanded and the work of governing, preaching and teaching grew, so the leadership gifts of men like Silas were increasingly recognized, and they were given key positions.

The same thing happened in the case of Stephen the first martyr, Philip the evangelist, and Barnabas the missionary. These men were not apostles appointed by God, but were leaders chosen by the church. To be put in a leadership rôle by one's fellow believers in the local church is a great privilege, and carries with it its own responsibilities and testings. One must then expect to become a focus of different attitudes of praise and blame, of encouragement and criticism, but it is all part of the cost of the privilege of having people put their trust in us.

To those in a leadership rôle in the local church, however modest, there are things we can keep in mind:

- we hold our position under God, so let us take it seriously and not let God down.

- we have been chosen by our fellow believers in the church, so let us not let the people down.

- we enjoy the privilege which goes with leadership, so let us not let ourselves down.

A gifted preacher

When Silas and Judas arrived at the church in Antioch and delivered the decision of the Jerusalem church, they also engaged in a ministry of preaching and teaching. 'Judas and Silas, who themselves were prophets, said much to encourage and strengthen the brothers' (v.32). The description 'prophets' is not used in the sense of 'foretelling' future events, but in the sense of 'forthtelling' or 'telling forth' the gospel of Christ. Both Silas and Judas were faithful in presenting the Word of God in all its fulness for the encouraging and strengthening of the church at Antioch.

Paul bears this out where Silas is concerned: 'For the Son of God, Jesus Christ, who was preached among you by me and Silas and Timothy, was not "Yes" and "No", but in him it has always been "Yes"' (2 Corinthians 1:18).

There Paul is saying that the preaching of Silas, Timothy and himself was not diffident and uncertain as though it was open-ended, being both 'yes' and 'no', but positive, clear and full of strong conviction. Later, Paul says: 'For no matter how many promises God has made, they are "Yes" in Christ' (2 Corinthians 1:20). That is the kind of preaching required in our churches today, instead of the uncertainty and woolly thinking that is so often paraded in our pulpits concerning the things of God. God's Word in his promises can be depended upon, simply because he is the unchanging God.

Silas was not the sort of preacher who left people swimming in a sea of question marks, as many preachers do today, so that the congregation is left asking: 'Do we address God as a he or a she? Is there a heaven and not a hell, or is there both or neither? Can I know for certain that my sins are forgiven and that I am at peace with God?' To all such questions, Silas' preaching would have given positive and clear answers.

Suffered for the faith

In Acts 16 we have an amazing picture of the hardships Paul and Silas suffered in the course of their missionary journeys: 'The crowd joined in the attack against Paul and Silas, and the magistrates ordered them to be stripped and beaten. After they had been severely flogged, they were thrown into prison and the jailer . . . put them in the inner cell and fastened their feet in the stocks. About midnight Paul and Silas were praying and singing hymns to God . . .' (v.22-5).

Here were two men with their backs raw and bleeding, incarcerated in a damp cold dungeon, with their feet in the stocks, and yet with a faith strong enough to praise God in prayer and song. It both amazes and humbles us, and clearly shows how willingly they paid the cost of that faith in terms of suffering.

It also raises the whole question of the depth and reality of our own faith and discipleship, and what it is costing us to belong to the Lord Jesus Christ. In our country we do not pay any cost in terms of physical suffering, but are we willing that our discipleship should make any demands upon us? Are we prepared that it should even put us to some personal inconvenience? Or have we got into the habit of enjoying a laid-back Christianity without effort, discipline, sacrifice or demand of any kind? Cost always imparts value to a thing, and that is true of our Christian faith. After all, it cost God his Son to save us, and in the light of that there is surely nothing too costly we can do for him in return?

20
Nathanael
a true seeker

Read John 1:45-51

A ll we know about Nathanael is to be found in this passage. It is not a lot, and yet it is sufficient to get inside his character and discover the kind of man he was. The background is the calling of the first disciples, Andrew, Peter and Philip.

Nathanael owed his faith to another

The passage opens with Philip going in search of Nathanael and introducing him to Jesus. 'Philip found Nathanael and told him, "We have found the one Moses wrote about in the Law, and about whom the prophets also wrote—Jesus of Nazareth, the son of Joseph"' (v.45). It was that word of personal evangelism by Philip that brought Nathanael to faith in Christ.

There are scores of books written today about evangelistic methods and the use of mime, drama, films, tapes and videos, not to mention the evangelistic rally. These, I have no doubt, can all be used in varying degrees to win others for Christ, but when all is said and done, the best method of all is one-to-one evangelism—one person in a simple friendly way talking to another about the Lord Jesus Christ. It may mean inviting that person into your home for coffee, or offering to pick them up to bring them to a gospel service.

But, in some way or other, personal contact needs to be made in a friendly and winsome manner. It is an undisputed fact, as different surveys have shown, that most people are won for Christ, not through the mass evangelistic rally, but through a neighbour, or a friend, or a colleague at work, speaking to them in a personal capacity about Christ, and inviting them to a church service where the gospel is preached. It was through Philip's personal witness to him that Nathanael came to faith.

Nathanael's lack of enthusiasm

But be warned! Personal evangelism is not easy. You can be snubbed or treated in a very offhand and indifferent way. Nathanael was not very enthusiastic when Philip first spoke to him about the Lord Jesus. Indeed, he was highly sceptical: 'Nazareth! "Can anything good come from there?" Nathanael asked' (v.46). He meant that Nazareth had never been remarkable in its history for anything. It had never produced a great leader or prophet, or had any outstanding spiritual associations. In fact, Nazareth isn't even mentioned in the Old Testament. How could anything good and worthwhile come out of a drab, insignificant, place like that?

In personal evangelism we must expect that kind of sceptical cynical reaction at times. 'What me! come to church?' 'You must be joking, what can I get there?' 'No, religion's all right for those who want it, but it's not for me'. We would be naïve to expect that people will respond enthusiastically to our overtures. After all, you are talking to them about something that is utterly strange, and which they have never even given a moment's serious thought to before. It all sounds fanciful and weird to them. So don't be put off by the cool cynical remark.

To those outside of Christ we must exercise wisdom and patience. Paul says: 'Be wise in the way you act towards outsiders; make the most of every opportunity. Let your conversation be always full of grace . . .' (Colossians 4:5,6). We must let people see that we are interested in them as persons in their own right and not simply as potential converts. Philip replied to Nathanael: 'Come and see', and he brought him to Jesus. That was very wise. He didn't argue with Nathanael, but invited him to put Christ and his message to the test for himself. That is what we must try to do. Put yourself out of the way to bring a person under the preaching of the gospel. Invite them to tea, ferry them to the service. Do anything, but get them there, and then leave it with the Lord and his Word to do the rest.

Nathanael—a man of integrity

But however sceptical Nathanael may have been about the possibility of the Messiah coming from a place like Nazareth, he was at least being honest. And that was in keeping with his character. He was a man of absolute integrity and transparent honesty. That was our Lord's estimate of him: 'When Jesus saw Nathanael approaching, he said of him, "Here is a true Israelite, in whom there is nothing false"' (v.47).

Nathanael was no hypocrite, that was why he had spoken his mind so openly and honestly to Philip. He was genuinely longing for the Messiah to come, and he wasn't going to be put off with facile explanations and answers that failed to satisfy his enquiring heart and mind for the truth of God's salvation. He was a true and sincere seeker and God always loves a seeker and will satisfy the longing of the heart that honestly pursues the truth. He did that for Nathanael, as is clear from his confession of faith in Christ.

Nathanael's confession

'"How do you know me?" Nathanael asked. Jesus answered, "I saw you while you were still under the fig-tree before Philip called you." Then Nathanael declared, "Rabbi, you are the Son of God; you are the King of Israel"' (v.48,49). There was no longer any doubt or scepticism in Nathanael's heart. What impressed him was that Jesus knew all about him, even the hidden things. He knew that the Lord Jesus was looking right into the depths of his heart, and knew all about his hopes and longings for truth and righteousness and for the coming of God's Messiah and Kingdom. What Jesus said about the fig-tree convinced him of that.

In Bible times, the fig-tree with its low leafy branches was often used as a place for prayer and meditation, because it was hidden from the prying eyes and distractions of the world around. But it was not hidden from the Lord. What is more, he knew what Nathanael was doing under the fig-tree, he knew his genuine longing concerning the promises of God for his people. That was what called out the confession of Nathanael, 'Rabbi, you are the Son of God . . .'

God in Christ knows all about us. 'I the Lord search the heart and examine the mind . . .' (Jeremiah 17:10). He knows us in a way that the prying inquisitive eyes of other people can never know us. He knows our true selves, our hopes and longings, our hidden sins and deceptions, our hidden fears and inadequacies. That knowledge, that God by his Spirit knows us so intimately, and yet still loves us and wants us for his own, is what should bring from us the confession that Jesus Christ alone is Saviour and Lord.

Greater things

But coming to know Christ as Saviour was only the beginning for Nathanael. There were greater things to come. 'Jesus said, "You believe, because I told you I saw you under the fig-tree. You shall see greater things than that." He then added, "I tell you the truth, you shall see heaven open, and the angels of God ascending and descending on the Son of Man"' (v.50,51).

Jesus was referring there to the Old Testament story (Genesis 28) of Jacob's dream, when he saw a ladder from earth to heaven, and the angels of God ascending and descending on it, and God spoke to him. Nathanael too would have greater experiences of God's power and presence, if he remained faithful. And so it is for all who come to faith in Christ. That is only the beginning. We can all go on to greater things. The communication between heaven and earth will become a greater reality, we can grow in understanding, and see greater truths concerning God's purpose for the Church and the world. We can go on to see more and more of God's glory in our lives, confirming us in our faith. And a day will indeed dawn when the heavens will open, and we shall see the Lord Jesus coming in glory and power to gather his own to himself, and to establish his kingdom in the new heaven and the new earth for all eternity.

21
Hymenaeus and Alexander
who shipwrecked their faith

Read 1 Timothy 1:18-20

In this chapter we are considering the characters of Hymenaeus and Alexander together because they share the same essential features in relation to the Christian faith and they are linked together by Paul in his letters to Timothy.

A shipwrecked faith

When Paul says to Timothy: 'Some . . . have shipwrecked their faith. Among them are Hymenaeus and Alexander' (v.19,20), I believe he spoke as much in sadness as in anger. For here were two men who had shown great promise in the Lord's work and had been able leaders in the church. In his second letter to Timothy, Paul mentions Hymenaeus again and refers to his teaching in conjunction with another church leader named Philetus: 'Their teaching will spread like gangrene. Among them are Hymenaeus and Philetus' (2 Timothy 2:17). Later, in the same letter, Paul refers to Alexander again and says that he was strongly opposed to the Christian message (2 Timothy 4:14). What he means is that Alexander, along with Hymenaeus, opposed the gospel with their own false teaching concerning the resurrection: 'They say that the resurrection has already taken place, and they destroy the faith of some' (2 Timothy 2:18).

Here were men therefore who had held influential positions in the church, so that Paul is led to make special mention of them when they made a shipwreck of their faith, and fell from the state of grace. It is always sad when a person makes a shipwreck of their faith, but it is particularly so when it happens to those in leadership positions, such as pastors and teachers. It can happen for many reasons, but in the loose sexual climate of today we hear of it happening all too often among pastors and church leaders, because of sexual sin. It is immensely serious when pastors and teachers are involved.

In the Letter of James we read this: 'Not many of you should presume to be teachers, my brothers, because you know that we who teach will be judged more strictly' (3:1). Anyone who claims to have been called of God to preach and teach his Word takes upon himself a profound responsibility, and will be held more accountable to God than others if he fails to live by the truth he teaches. After all, how can a weak man teach others to be strong?

But it is especially serious when a church leader makes a shipwreck of his faith, because it can have a disastrous effect upon the faith of others under his care. That is why Paul was so angry with Hymenaeus and Alexander—he says 'they destroy the faith of some' (2 Timothy 2:18). When people look to a pastor or teacher to be their guide in holy things, it can have a deeply disillusioning and cynical effect when they see that same person making a shipwreck of the very faith he taught. They are likely to think that you can't trust the spiritual integrity of anyone, not even ministers of the gospel. Anyone in a leadership position in the church therefore, and that would include Sunday school teachers and youth leaders as well as pastors, needs to guard his faith and personal testimony very closely in today's world. Paul's words in another context are appropriate here: 'So, if you

think you are standing firm, be careful that you don't fall!'
(1 Corinthians 10:12).

How does it happen?

People make a shipwreck of their faith for many and varied
reasons. And we are thinking now, not especially of church
leaders, but of Christians in general. Some fall into sexual sin
and ruin their Christian character and testimony. It may also
mean the ruin of home and marriage, and a great deal of un-
happiness for those closest to them. It can happen because of
some traumatic experience through which a person passes,
such as a sudden bereavement which makes them bitter and
deeply resentful towards God, and their faith simply col-
lapses. For others, it can be material success that gradually
takes the place of spiritual things, and God gets left out of the
picture. With young Christians, it can happen when they
leave home to go to college or to work elsewhere. With their
new-found freedom and away from the Christian restraints
and influences that had supported them previously, they get
caught up in wrong company and, before they know it, their
faith is on the rocks, and their Christian life a miserable shipwreck.

But more important than *how* it happens is *why* it happens.
In the case of Hymenaeus and Alexander, the reason is clear.
Paul says of Hymenaeus and Philetus that they 'wandered
away from the truth' (2 Timothy 2:18). He says of Alexander
that 'he strongly opposed our message', meaning the message of the truth in Christ (4:15). Both had got caught up in
false teaching concerning the resurrection (2:18) claiming
that a person is resurrected spiritually, but can have no hope
of a future resurrection of the body. Paul says significantly
that such false teaching 'will spread like gangrene' (2:17),

thus causing them and others to wander further and further from the truth.

Medically speaking, gangrene has a corrupting effect, which spreads like a poison through the whole system. Hymenaeus and Alexander had corrupted and perverted the doctrine of the resurrection, and substituted man-made ideas in place of the Word of God. In so doing they had made a shipwreck of their own lives and that of others by causing them to 'wander from the truth'. The moment that happens, and people move away from the truth of God's Word revealed in the Scriptures, they become like a ship without a rudder, and their faith will soon be on the rocks and totally shipwrecked.

It is a sad fact that today we are seeing quite a lot of wandering from the truth of God's Word in the Scriptures, and people's faith is undoubtedly suffering. Ours is an age in which the authority of the Bible is no longer accepted, even by pastors and teachers in the Church, and the doctrinal truths that once served to anchor people's faith have been jettisoned. All too often, man-made ideas are substituted for the truth of God's Word and the teaching of the Bible is distorted and manipulated to fit modern scientific and humanistic thinking. Such truths, as the resurrection, the virgin birth, the deity of Christ, the reality of hell and the judgment, are frequently denied, along with the miraculous element in the Bible.

The consequence of this 'wandering from the truth' has meant that the faith of ordinary Christian people in our churches has been seriously affected for the worse. Instead of being fed in their souls by those who are meant to be their shepherds, they are being starved of spiritual understanding and continue to wander further and further from the truth, until eventually their faith is shipwrecked on the rocks of unbelief.

Referring to Alexander, Paul warns Timothy: 'You too should be on your guard against him, because he strongly opposed our message' (2 Timothy 4:15). In the same way we need to guard against those false teachings that would destroy our faith. We need to be discriminating and discerning in the kind of preaching we hear from the pulpit, the books and magazine articles that appear under the guise of 'evangelical'; and we need to bring everything to the bar of the Word of God in Holy Scripture. There are so many teaching 'fads' in evangelical circles today and the only safe way to prevent one's faith from being shipwrecked is to take the Bible as our rudder to help us follow a steady and true course.

Church discipline

There is still one other things that Paul says about Hymenaeus and Alexander, and it is the most serious and frightening thing of all: 'Among them are Hymenaeus and Alexander, whom I have handed over to Satan to be taught not to blaspheme' (1 Timothy 1:20).

What does Paul mean by 'handed over to Satan'? Bible scholars are generally agreed that it certainly involved being put out of the local church—that is expulsion from the church fellowship as a form of discipline. We notice that the reason given is that they should 'be taught [disciplined] not to blaspheme'. It is detestable for the Christian when the names of God and Christ are heard being blasphemed on television as often as we do. But Paul has something even worse in mind than that. The worst of all blasphemies is to deny or reject the truth of God and his Word. That is what Hymenaeus and Alexander did. Paul says to them in effect: 'Since you reject the truth of God's Word as the rule of life, then you must leave the church, and we hand you over to the rule of the great rejecter himself, Satan, and we hope that this will discipline you and bring you to your senses so that you will not reject God's truth any longer.'

Paul is telling us that when a man rejects the truth of God's Word, he is committing the ultimate blasphemy since he is rejecting God himself and deliberately making himself the willing tool and instrument of Satan. It is also reminding us as Christians of the need for discipline in the Church. In many churches, even those who call themselves evangelical, things are tolerated that bring the gospel of Jesus Christ into disrepute. We seem to have gone soft on discipline in today's churches and in this we are simply following a trend that is characteristic of secular society rather than the New Testament Church.

22
Onesiphorus
a refreshing character

Read 2 Timothy 1:16-18

A ll that we know of Onesiphorus is to be found in these three verses apart from the mere mention of his name in 4:19. The name means 'profitable' and from the commendation given him by Paul in these verses he certainly found Onesiphorus to be just that—profitable and someone worth knowing as a fellow believer and a friend.

Christian winsomeness

To appreciate the depth of feeling with which Paul spoke the words of commendation: 'May the Lord show mercy to the household of Onesiphorus because he often refreshed me and was not ashamed of my chains' (v.16), we have to realize that he was in prison for a second time and was expecting shortly to face death, 'the time has come for my departure' (4:6). It is against that dark background that Paul speaks so warmly of the winsome, lovely character of Onesiphorus, who refreshed his spirit by visiting him in prison. Moreover it seems that Onesiphorus had been in the habit of carrying out a similar ministry of 'refreshment' in the church at Ephesus: 'You know very well in how many ways he helped me in Ephesus' (v.18).

In what way did he refresh Paul's spirit in prison? First of all, by simply visiting him and showing that he was not forgotten by his Christian friends. Even great men like the apostle can get low in spirits and need the ministry of refreshment from time to time. John Bunyan, that mighty saint of God, gives us an insight into how he felt at certain low points in his experience in Bedford jail.

> When I first came into prison I was bold in God. I preached in the prison, and many a time there stirred within me that which is like the burden of the old prophets of God. I printed many books that, blessed be God, have been a benefit to many, but when in the dark of the night I lay on my straw, and was wellnigh stifled by the heat, I was like one borne down with my thoughts, and started as if stung when I thought of my dear ones, alone in the world . . . But I rose above those sorrows, like a bird that goes high over the clouds into the clear sunlight of God, and in the main I kept the peace of Christ.

We can imagine therefore how cheered and refreshed Paul must have been by the visit of Onesiphorus. He would have brought the apostle food and drink and news of the church at Ephesus. But the question as to *how* he refreshed Paul is less important than the fact that he *did* refresh him. There are some dear people in whose company we feel ourselves drained and emptied, but there are others, like Onesiphorus, who brace us up and come like a breath of fresh air into our lives.

The ministry of refreshment

The ministry of refreshment is one that is always needed somewhere and can be exercised by a true Christian. If a believer, who knows the warmth and love of Christ in his heart, cannot revive and refresh the spirits of those who are fatigued and discouraged with life, then who can? After all, this is the ministry that doesn't call for any special gift or talent, such as being a good speaker, or having a good singing voice, or a first-class intellect. It is simply a matter of Christian disposition. How do we do it?

First, we refresh people when we attempt to get alongside them in their distresses and show the fruit of the Spirit in 'love, joy, peace, patience, kindness'. In Paul's words we are to 'be kind and compassionate to one another' (Ephesians 4:32). That is what Onesiphorus was doing for him— being kind and compassionate. In verse 17, Paul says of Onesiphorus: 'when he was in Rome, he searched hard for me until he found me'. We must imagine this gracious, lovely, winsome man travelling all the way from Asia, when he hears that Paul was in prison in Rome. He hasn't a clue where to find him, but day after day, with grim determination, he roams the streets of the great city, asking questions and gleaning every bit of information he can, until eventually he finds him. There was no special talent or great genius involved in that! It was a simple ministry of kindness and compassion, and a determination on the part of Onesiphorus not to give up until he had searched out Paul and brought some refreshment to his soul and spirit. What is there to prevent us doing that for some one?

Second, we refresh people in their spirit, when we speak words of encouragement to them. Eliphaz, the friend of Job, said to him: 'Your words have supported those who stumbled; you have strengthened faltering knees' (Job 4:4). We can do that when we get alongside the new convert and help him to a clearer understanding of his faith, or when we engage in writing to a missionary on a regular basis, or when we help a backslider to be restored, or when we pray with someone who is emotionally shattered by some experience which they have passed through.

Not ashamed of Christ

Paul says not only that Onesiphorus had refreshed him in his spirit but that he 'was not ashamed of my chains'. That remark stands in sharp contrast with what he says about two other Christians in the previous verse: 'You know that everyone in the province of Asia has deserted me, including Phygelus and Hermogenes' (v.15). What he means is that these two men, unlike Onesiphorus, were ashamed of his chains; that they would not identify with him as a Christian leader, because that was a dangerous thing to do. This was the age of the Roman Emperor Nero, who put so many believers to death. Onesiphorus was clearly putting his life in danger by seeking out Paul and visiting him in prison.

There is a risk element still in being a follower of the Lord Jesus, even if it only be a risk to our popularity with others, or to our reputation, or to our chances of promotion at work. It is negligible compared with the risk that Onesiphorus was taking in getting alongside Paul, but are we willing to be even that daring for the cause of the gospel?

The eternal reward

Paul concludes what he was saying about Onesiphorus with devout prayer and wish that 'he will find mercy from the Lord on that day!' He means, of course, the Judgment Day. But he is not praying that Onesiphorus will receive salvation for his soul on that day since, as a believer, that was already assured through Christ. Paul means that by God's mercy Onesiphorus will be rewarded for his own merciful and godly conduct in this life. The implication may be that this godly man had already died and gone to his eternal reward.

Scripture clearly teaches that at the Judgment Day believers will be rewarded for the quality of their Christian discipleship here below. The Lord Jesus spoke frequently of rewards, and how deeds, small and great, performed in this life will not be forgotten, but will be recalled and rewarded in heaven. 'Anyone who gives you a cup of water in my name . . . will certainly not lose his reward' (Mark 9:41). 'For the Son of Man is going to come in his Father's glory with his angels, and then he will reward each person according to what he has done' (Matthew 16:27). Speaking in the same vein of the assessment of the Christian's work and discipleship in heaven, Paul says: 'If what he has built survives, he will receive his reward' (1 Corinthians 3:14).

All this emphasizes the need to take our Christian discipleship seriously, and seek to emulate Onesiphorus in his winsomeness of character and godly service, so that God in his great mercy may reward us abundantly on that Great Day.

23
Gaius
Diotrephes, Demetrius
—three men and the truth

Read 3 John

In this brief letter of just fourteen verses, it is striking how often the 'truth' is referred to in connection with the three personalities we are considering. In verse 1 John speaks of loving the truth; in verses 3 and 4 walking in the truth; in verse 8 working for the truth; in verses 9 and 10 hindering the truth; and in verse 12 commending the truth.

In his opening greeting to Gaius, John addresses him as a friend and fellow believer whom he loves 'in the truth', the truth of their common salvation in Christ. Our love for one another as brothers and sisters in the family of God flows from the experience of the truths we share in our acceptance of the gospel. We have been cleansed by the same work of God's grace; we are indwelt by the same Holy Spirit; we have the same glorious hope of the return of Christ to gather his own and the same expectation of eternal life in heaven. These are the common bonds of truth that explain the special love we have for one another. As the hymn says:

> *Blest be the tie that binds*
> *Our hearts in Christian love;*
> *The fellowship of kindred minds*
> *Is like to that above.*

Gaius, who walked in the truth

We have no idea how Gaius first became a Christian, since the only details we have concerning his life are those found in this personal letter from John. However, it is likely that he came to an understanding of the truth of Christ through John's ministry, since we learn from verses 3,4 that he continues to 'walk in the truth', and that John has 'no greater joy than to hear that my children are walking in the truth.' Clearly, Gaius was a product or child of John's ministry in the truth of God's Word.

What does it mean to 'walk in the truth'? It means to live in obedience to the truth of the gospel, which we have accepted through faith. To 'walk in the truth' is to advance in godly living and to make progress in Christian understanding. Gaius, it would seem, was doing just that, he was working out his faith in the practicalities of daily life. We are reminded of Paul's words to the Philippian believers: 'continue to work out your salvation with fear and trembling, for it is God who works in you to will and to act according to his good purpose' (2:12).

The Christian life is more than the acceptance of the truth of God in Christ. When we have done that, we then have to work out that truth of salvation in the way we live, otherwise our Christian faith is no more than an intellectual truth, something we have grasped with the mind, mere head knowledge. The truth must show itself in the way we behave, in our life-style, our conversation, in the way we spend our money, the kind of pleasures we enjoy and so on. It is interesting to read in verse 2 that John is glad to hear that Gaius enjoys good health in body, but he is even more pleased that his 'soul is getting along well.'

People sometimes say: 'Good health is everything.' That is

not true. Health of body is extremely important, but it is by no means everything. More important even than health of body is the health of the soul, for that *is* everything. 'What good will it be for a man if he gains the whole world [including good health], yet forfeits his soul? Or what can a man give in exchange for his soul?' (Matthew 16:26).

Gaius showed his health of soul and that his priorities were right by the way he demonstrated the love of God in the hospitality of his home towards the travelling missionaries or evangelists of the early Church (v.5-8). Here were men who couldn't look to the pagan world for back-up and support in the work of preaching the gospel. They were totally dependent upon Christians like Gaius being willing to practise their faith by opening their homes to provide hospitality.

That principle still holds good. We cannot look to the world to provide the necessary support for God's work. The whole idea of 'efforts', 'raffles', 'sales of work' and the like to finance the work of the church and the preaching of the gospel ought to be anathema to any true evangelical believer. God's work should be supported by God's people through the regular freewill offerings and other straight giving. This too, is an important aspect of what it means to 'walk in the truth', and to work out our salvation at the practical level.

Diotrephes, who hindered the truth

As Christian believers we can get terribly upset and disillusioned by the tensions and personality clashes that can arise in our church fellowships. But we must never forget that, even in the church, we are dealing with sinful human nature, and that the New Testament fellowships were no different. If all the members in our churches were like Gaius, then the pastor's job would be a sheer joy, and the work of the gospel would be one great forward movement. But the Devil sees to it that that is not the case, and every fellowship will have one or more Diotrephes, those who consciously or unconsciously do the Devil's work for him and who are a hindrance to the truth of Christ. John touches on three weaknesses in the character of Diotrephes.

In the first place, he was the victim of pride and of an inordinate sense of his own importance: 'Diotrephes, who loves to be first' (v.9). That was his chief weakness, a love of prominence and the up-front position. Clearly, he was a man of strong personality, and he seems to have held some office of authority in the fellowship, possibly an elder, or he may even have been the pastor, since he excommunicated members who gave a welcome to the visiting evangelists (v.10). Whatever his position, he was eaten up with pride and envy, and jealous of his own reputation. He was a man who knew very little about dying to self. Pride is the darling sin, and God can do nothing with the proud man except one thing— humble him! And that can be a very hurtful experience.

Secondly, he was a man who resisted authority and had an unteachable spirit. 'I wrote to the church, but Diotrephes . . . will have nothing to do with us.' This was John the apostle speaking, but such apostolic authority meant nothing to an unteachable spirit like Diotrephes. This seems to be widespread in today's evangelical churches—an unteachable spirit and a growing resistance to authority, even the authority of Scripture. There seem to be a growing number of people who think they know more and can lead better, and they are averse to being taught out of God's Word by those in pastoral office. Could this be a major factor in the fragmentation of congregations we are witnessing so much of today, and the desire to 'establish' a church or fellowship at the drop of a hat?

Then he was a man with a dangerous tongue. 'I will call attention to what he is doing, gossiping maliciously about us.' In conversation, Diotrephes would drop the tainted hint about John's leadership, or make the little innuendo about his character, or question his motives. What pastor is there who doesn't know something of that!

Such folk are real 'stirrers' in the fellowship, causing instability and discontent and they are a positive hindrance to the advancement of the truth of the gospel. Gossips are those who, with their drops of poison, can assassinate in five minutes a character that has taken thirty years or more to build. It was John's intention to discipline Diotrephes, and he has no hesitation in describing his conduct as evil, warning Gaius to stay well clear of him: 'Dear friend, do not imitate what is evil, but what is good' (v.11).

Demetrius, commended by the truth

'Demetrius is well spoken of by everyone—and even by the truth itself. We also speak well of him, and you know that our testimony is true' (v.12). It is good to have the testimony of others to one's faith and character. It is even better to have that testimony backed up by a trusted and authoritative source like John, but best of all is the testimony of the truth itself. John could only have meant that the reality of the truth of God and the internal witness of the Holy Spirit was transparently evident in the life and character of Demetrius. He was commended by the truth.

That surely is what God wants of all of us. Is it transparently evident to others with whom we live and work that our life is totally surrendered to Christ? Does the truth and reality of our salvation and commitment to the things of God come shining through? Remember Paul's words: 'For me to live, is

Christ'. Is that the message others get from us, that the driving force of our life is our Christian faith, and the only explanation for the kind of people we are is the Holy Spirit within us? It's a big question.

24
Timothy
a true son in the faith

Read 2 Timothy 1:3-5 and 3:14,15

In one sense, Timothy can hardly be described as one of the lesser-known characters of the New Testament, since there are two Letters, written by Paul, which bear his name. Nevertheless, although these Letters are well known, what do we know about the man himself, his character and personality, and the part he played in the formation of the early Church?

A godly upbringing

From Acts 16:1 we learn that Timothy came from Lystra, a Roman colony, that his mother was a Jewess and a believer, but that his father was an unbeliever and a Greek Gentile. Timothy grew up to be a powerful advocate for the gospel and a fellow-missionary of the apostle Paul, mainly because of the Christian groundwork done in his life as a child. 'I have been reminded of your sincere faith, which first lived in your grandmother Lois and in your mother Eunice and, I am persuaded, now lives in you also' (1:5). 'From infancy you have known the holy Scriptures, which are able to make you wise for salvation through faith in Christ Jesus' (3:15).

Timothy's father, as an unbeliever, had no part in his spiritual upbringing, but his grandmother and mother were determined, in spite of that, to see to it that he was grounded thoroughly in the things of God.

In the increasingly secular society of today, it is an enormously difficult task to provide our children with a Christian upbringing, and when we reflect on the growing number of one-parent families, or homes where there is no interest or support from the father, then the burden is even greater. But God gives grace even in that situation, as is evident from the way it was handled by Timothy's mother and grandmother in the pagan world of New Testament times. The reason for this is because that is how God wants our children to be brought up. From Genesis to Revelation the Bible lays tremendous emphasis on the rôle of the family for godliness of life. This is clearly seen from such exhortations as: 'Honour your father and your mother' (Exodus 20:12). 'Train a child in the way he should go, and when he is old he will not turn from it' (Proverbs 22:6). 'Fathers, do not exasperate your children, instead, bring them up in the training and instruction of the Lord' (Ephesians 6:4).

Today, in spite of the tremendous influence of television and school upon our children, the home is still the place where the real spadework is done in the instilling of spiritual values which will help them to come to faith in the Lord Jesus Christ. A home and a family without any Godward direction leaves itself open to all the corrupting influences which are so evident today: crime, violence, drunkeness, drug-addiction and sexual immorality. The Christian parent may at times be tempted to ask whether it is wise even to have children in a degenerate world like ours. The biblical answer to that is that the power of God's grace is always available to Christian parents. Eunice and Lois are proof of that in the way that they brought up Timothy to love the things of God in the midst of a pagan world.

Coming to faith

But when all is said and done there is a limit to what Christian parents can do for their children spiritually. They can prepare the child for the Christian life, but the ultimate responsibility for entering into a personal relationship with Christ as Lord and Saviour falls upon the child himself. It would seem that Timothy, when a young man, became a Christian under the preaching and influence of the apostle Paul. In the first letter to Timothy Paul begins with the words: 'To Timothy my true son in the faith'. This can only mean that Timothy came to birth in Christ under Paul's ministry. Later, when Paul made a further visit to Lystra, Timothy had made progress in his faith and already had a personal testimony among the Christians there. 'The brothers at Lystra and Iconium spoke well of him. Paul wanted to take him along on the journey . . .' (Acts 16:2,3). So highly was Timothy thought of by the Christian community that Paul had no hesitation, it would seem, in taking him on as an assistant on his missionary travels.

There are two things we can note in all this. Each of us is personally responsible for our relationship with the Lord Jesus Christ. We may come from a godly home as Timothy did, and we can thank God for that. But faith has to be a personal experience, and like Timothy we have to have a personal testimony of what God has done in our lives. Secondly, Timothy's life is a reminder to young people to commit their life to Christ when they are still young. Young people may have a tendency to feel that, with all life stretching out before them, they can afford to leave such serious matters as their soul's destiny to a later time. But there *is* no later time. The only time we have is now and there is no guarantee that we have years ahead of us. More than that, God wants the vitality and energy and enthusiasm that youth can give in his service.

D. L. Moody, the evangelist, said after a meeting that he had had two-and-a-half professions of faith that night. Someone said: 'you mean two adults and a child?' Moody replied: 'No, I mean two young people and an adult.' He was right in the sense that when a person commits their life to Christ in adulthood, it is only half a life, since the other half has already been spent. When a life is handed over to God at an early age, there is no knowing what great things God might do with it. Timothy went on to become a missionary, a church leader and a pastor.

Low self-image

When we read carefully all the references to Timothy by Paul, we get the impression that he was the very opposite of the dynamic, aggressive, positive personality that is so often associated with Christian leadership today. The picture we get is of a rather diffident, hesitant, timid kind of man, something of an introvert with a very low self-image and rather sickly into the bargain.

Let us look at some of the references: 'For this reason, I remind you to fan into flame the gift of God, which is in you . . . For God did not give us a spirit of timidity, but a spirit of power, of love and of self-discipline' (2 Timothy 1:6,7). Timothy had a tendency to 'shrink' from the demands ministry made upon him and to be a bit fearful. He needed a bit of prodding from time to time, and Paul has to remind him to get a grip on himself and remember that the Holy Spirit imparts power, love, strength and self-discipline.

This same tendency to timidity and fearfulness comes through again when Paul writes to the church at Corinth. 'If Timothy comes, see to it that he has nothing to fear while he is with you . . .' (1 Corinthians 16:10). Paul knew that there were some difficult, overbearing people in the Corinthian church, and he seems to be saying: 'Go easy on young Timothy, you know how he hates confrontation.' Then again Paul says to him: 'Don't let anyone look down on you because you are young' (1 Timothy 4:12). Was Timothy in the habit of allowing folk to undermine his authority as a pastor?

And add to all this the fact that he was a sickly man physically. 'Stop drinking only water, and use a little wine because of your stomach and your frequent illnesses' (1 Timothy 5:23). It is sometimes thought that Timothy suffered from stress symptoms. Being a pastor and church leader in the pagan world was not easy for someone of his self-effacing disposition, and it may all have got on top of him at times.

What does all this say to us? Well, it shows us that, in spite of his personality problems and his obvious lack of those dynamic qualities we usually associate with leadership, Timothy was nevertheless greatly used of God. He had the one quality that really matters in the end—a deep love for God which overcame all his fears. In reading the Scriptures one is constantly amazed at some of the people God used in a leadership rôle; people like Jacob, a wily character; Aaron, who unlike his brother Moses, was rather weak; Jephthah, a social misfit and gang leader; Samson, a hot-headed impulsive man.

The fact is we can easily get this whole question of self-image and leadership potential out of perspective if we are not careful. On the one hand, we can have an inflated image of our abilities and see ourselves as competent, positive and ideal leadership material, when in actual fact we are none of these things in the eyes of others. 'If anyone thinks he is something when he is nothing, he deceives himself' (Galatians 6:3). But even if we do have these natural qualities, we still require the humility to keep it in perspective if God is to use us.

Likewise, we must be careful not to go to the other extreme, and have such a low self-image that we become spiritually paralysed where God's work is concerned. We can then be so negative as to think that we can contribute nothing, and thus we lack the expectancy that God can work through us in spite of our deficiences. A deep love for the Lord and a sense of total dependency upon him alone is what really matters in the end.

Recent books from the

Evangelical Press of Wales

Voices from the Welsh Revival 1904-05
Brynmor P. Jones

Drawing upon the testimonies of eye-witnesses, letters and diaries of those on the spot, newspaper reports and accounts in the periodicals of the time, Brynmor Jones presents a gripping account of the religious revival which so moved Wales at the beginning of this century. 304pp.

Pursued by God
A selective translation with notes of the Welsh religious classic Theomemphus by Williams Williams of Pantycelyn
Eifion Evans

This remarkable work displays profound insight into the Scriptures and a deep discernment in the realm of Christian experience in times of spiritual revival. 191pp.

Fire in the Thatch
the true nature of religious revival
Eifion Evans

This collection of the author's writings on the subject of revival clearly shows the true nature of God's visitations of his people, particularly though not exclusively in Wales. 238pp.

Taught to Serve
The history of the Barry and Bryntirion Colleges
Noel Gibbard

Dr Gibbard traces the development of the present Evangelical Theological College of Wales from the years following the Revival of 1904–05. Essential reading for all seeking an understanding of the ministry of evangelicalism in Wales during this century. 256pp.

Christian Preachers
Nigel Clifford

From Chrysostom and Augustine to A. W. Tozer and Martyn Lloyd-Jones in this century this book introduces us to the lives and achievements of thirty-one outstanding preachers of the Christian Church. 320pp.
'For lovers of the gift of preaching, this book has much to offer'—*Evangelism Today*

Books by
Dr D. Martyn Lloyd-Jones
from the Evangelical Press of Wales

Out of the Depths

An exposition of Psalm 51 which deals
with the problem of human failure and guilt and
the divine remedy of repentance. 70pp.

'A mine of practical application and
pastoral wisdom. It will humble
and uplift.'—*Gospel Magazine*

Why Does God Allow War?

An honest and sympathetic treatment of the
question, Why does God seem not to answer
the prayers of his people in the face of
evil and suffering? 128pp.

'Readers finding themselves facing trials
will find these sermons instructive and
relevant.'—*Bible League Quarterly*

Truth Unchanged, Unchanging

A powerful examination of life's fundamental
questions, and a penetrating biblical
diagnosis of the nature of man, so
different from modern views. 125pp.

Water in the Desert

An evangelistic sermon pointing to
the only source of true happiness
and fulfilment. 20pp.

NOTES

NOTES

NOTES